Loretta Santini

CITIES OF ITALY

VENICE

GUIDE WITH PLAN

Published and printed by

NARNI - TERNI

AN OVERALL VIEW

Venice is one of the best-known and best-loved cities of the world. The reason for this lies in the extraordinary beauty of its monuments and its art treasures, and in its history. But above all, it is to be found in the special quality which is reflected in the waters of its canals and side-channels, with the churches and palaces scattered around dozens of islands and islets in the Lagoon. Venice lives its life in an atmosphere of enchantment and fable, with a touch of melancholy added. What astonishes the visitor most of all is the strange image of a duplicated city: its churches and monuments are seen reversed in the waters of the canals, and become evanescent, shifting, everchanging. They line the banks of the Grand Canal, following its broad sinuous curves with their facades of the finest lace-like carving. Silence permeates the rios and calle, and the most secluded little squares of the city. The enchanted fascination of the rich architecture or the mosaics of San Marco shimmering in the sun, and the magnificent mansions such as the Doges' Palace, or the Ca' d'Oro or the Ca' Pesaro, gives the city an air of opulent splendour, and causes it to gleam and sparkle. And the Rialto Bridge, the Bridge of Sighs, the superb architecture of Longhena, Sansovino and Scarpagnino, the great paintings of Tiepolo, Tintoretto and the delicate work of Bellini, the sculptures of the Lombardos, the decorations in the full flower of Gothic art, all go to make Venice one of the unique and unforgettable cities of the world.

BRIEF HISTORICAL NOTES

The Venetian lagoon was inhabited from the 5th century of the Christian era, when as a result of the barbarian invasions, the peoples of the hinterland were forced to take refuge on the thousands of little islands which face out to the Adriatic. Here they built a community under the leadership of a 'Dux' (to be known as the Doge in the future), who was initially chosen by the Emperor, and was subject to him. From the eighth century onwards, however, the Doge came to be chosen by popular assemblies, and this opened the way to the political and institutional autonomy of the city. It was from this period that the fortunes of the future Republic of Venice began: from the tenth to the eleventh centuries, thanks to its strategic geographical position, and the skill and initiative of its inhabitants, the city became the centre of trade in the Adriatic, and later the queen of the trade-routes to the East, assuming the role of a front rank mercantile power.

This meant that enormous riches flowed in. It was then that Venice built the splendid monuments which are its chief characteristic today: the finest churches and the grandest palazzi rose, and this was the moment of the greatest cre-

ative flowering of painters, sculptors and architects. The sea and the trade routes were the very life of Venice. Marco Polo, merchant-venturer, embodies better than anyone the characteristics of the people of the city. Having reached China and lived there for some time, he was to narrate in "Il Milione" the story of his travels and the customs of that land. From the sixteenth century onwards the maritime role of the city diminished, as the main focus of trade was turned from the East to the West. Despite this, the Republic would always have a leading place in the economy and history of the Italian peninsula. It was to remain independent until 1799, when as a result of the Treaty of Campoformio it became part of the Kingdom of Lombardy and Venetia, and was then ceded to Austria. From 1866 onward, it became part of the new united Kingdom of Italy.

Photo above: Gondolas making their way down the canals of Venice.
Photo below: The Procession of the Cross in St Mark's Square (1496): Gentile Bellini. This is a beautiful painting in the Accademia Gallery of Venice. It shows one of the most moving moments of the religious ceremonies held in the great central square of Venice to honour of the reliquary of the Cross.

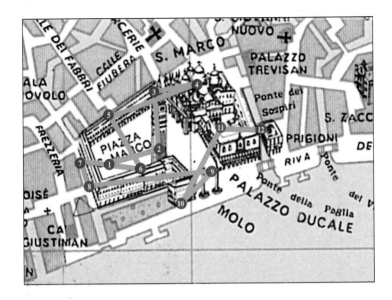

1. PIAZZA SAN MARCO

This is the religious, historical and social centre of the city. At one time it was also its political hub.

Thanks to its harmonious elegance, its beauty and its monuments, it is rightly considered the great "salotto" of Venice. It is a very large area, trapezoidal in shape and measuring 175.50 metres (nearly 580 feet) in length and 82 (266 feet) in width. Its natural continuation is in the nearby Piazzetta San Marco, which lies between the Doges' Palace, the Libreria and the Pier.

The piazza took on its present shape in the sixteenth century, when the architect Sansovino drew up its basic design. It is closed in on its longer sides by the Old Law Courts and the Clock Tower on the one hand, and by the New Law Courts on the other. On the shorter sides stand the so-called "New Building" or former Royal Palace, and above all the stupendous Basilica of San Marco flanked by the massive Campanile.

2. THE CAMPANILE OF SAN MARCO AND SANSOVINO'S LOGGETTA

Almost 100 metres high, this splendid tower stands beside the Basilica of San Marco. Built towards the end of the ninth century, it was extended in height in the twelfth, and rebuilt several times, being completed at the beginning of the sixteenth century. In 1902 it suffered a disastrous collapse, and was rebuilt a few years later as an exact replica of the original.

4

Panoramic view of the monuments on St Mark's Basin.

Sansovino's loggetta: an elegant piece of Renaissance architecture built in the mid 16th century.

The architecture shows the various phases of its construction: it has Romanesque elements in the lower section, and Renaissance features in the upper part. On the topmost point stands a gilded Angel, which turns on its own axis. The bells which once occupied the belfry of the campanile had various names according to the notes that they were destined to give out, for example the principal hours of the day or the sentences of the Court. The ascent to the top of the campanile (which has a conveniently designed spiral staircase and a lift) provides the chance to enjoy a broad panorama over Venice and its lagoon.

THE LOGGETTA OF SANSOVINO

Standing at the foot of the Campanile, and a real gem of Renaissance architecture, the loggetta was designed by Sansovino in the early part of the 16th century. The front is punctuated by three rounded arches flanked by columns. Lower down there is a balustrade which is mirrored in the attic section. Fine bronze statues of Minerva, Apollo, Mercury and Peace have been inserted into the niches, and the marble ornaments decorating the upper front section are very fine.

3.THE CLOCK TOWER

Built to a design by Coducci towards the end of the fifteenth century, it is famous for the two Moors which strike the hours on the great bell.

The clock is made up of a quadrant which indicates the movement of the sun and the moon and the signs of the Zodiac. When the hour strikes, a procession of figures made up of Angels and Wise Men bows towards the Madonna and Child.1.

The clock tower: This work of Coducci at the end of the 15th century is best known for the two Moors who beat out the hours on the huge bell.

4. THE BASILICA OF SAN MARCO

HISTORY

The Church was built in the mid-eleventh century to enshrine the body of the Evangelist St Mark, which had been brought to Venice in the year 829. Previously another building had stood on the site, and this in turn had replaced an even more ancient one, destroyed by a fire. The consecration took place in 1094. From that moment, the basilica was constantly embellished with an exceptional series of works of art - a great deal of it was taken, in fact, from other ancient buildings, and the finest of all was its magnificent and unique series of mosaics. In a very few years, the church became one of the most beautiful, theatrical and grandiose basilicas of all time. The building is in the form of a Greek cross, with four domes placed above each branch, and a larger central dome at the crossing. An atrium has been added to the front, which continues around the two sides as far as the transversal wings. The style of the Basilica has a strong Byzantine flavour, but Romanesque and Renaissance architecture also play their part, and this mingling, together with the rich decoration, renders the overall effect absolutely unique. The architect of the building is unknown. However, it is certain that the complex was the product of constant labour by artists and master-craftsmen, who each contributed, in his own sector, to the splendour of this basilica, and despite the diversities of style, to giving it a unity in conception.

THE FACADE

The facade stands out for the magnificence of its architecture, the splendour of the mosaics as they glitter in the sun, and the

perfect delicacy of the filigree decorations which frame every element and rise to a climax in the crowning of the arches.

THE LOWER PART

Five great doorways open from the facade, the central one being the tallest. They are adorned with clusters of marble columns, which give a strong effect of mobility. The bas-reliefs which decorate them

The Basilica of San Marco: overall view of the facade. This is one of the most important monuments of past ages, and also one of the most valuable and interesting, thanks to its rich decoration and the masterpieces which are contained in it.

(especially those of the central door) are absolute masterpieces of Romanesque carving, and recount *Sacred histories*, and *Episodes of everyday life, the Months, and the Occupations of Mankind*. The final arch, towards the south, has been closed off in order to create the Zen Chapel and the Baptistery.

THE UPPER PART

This repeats the five arches of the lower order. The central arch, taller again than the others, has a window which illuminates the interior of the Basilica. This is where the group of *Four Horses* in bronze is to be found, a masterpiece of Greek sculpture of the 4th-3rd centuries BC. They were brought to Venice in 1204 by Doge Enrico Dandolo, after the (Venetian) conquest of Constantinople. The *Chariot* has on several occasions been removed from Venice because of its value and beauty; Napoleon ordered it to be carried off to Paris in 1798 in order to place it in front of the Tuileries. In the arches flanking the central one are four great mosaics created in the sixteenth century to the design of Maffeo da Verona. They portray: *The Deposition of Christ from the Cross, the Descent into Hell; The Resurrection of Christ, The Ascension into Heaven*. The sculptures of the upper section are among the most important masterpieces of Gothic art. On the summit of the Basilica is the statue of *St Mark*, and the *Lion of Saint Mark*.

SOUTH SIDE

This repeats the pattern of the facade, with its fine rows of arches one above the other. Here can be seen the so-called *Acritan Pilasters*, their title deriving from the fact that they were brought to Venice from San John of Acre after the victory over Genova there in 1256. They are priceless examples of Syrian art of the sixth century. The group of the *Tetrarchs* should also be noted: two pairs of warriors, almost certainly portraying the Emperors Diocletian, Maximilianus, Valerius and Constans. This is a fourth century work, probably Syrian, though some ascribe it to Egypt.

NORTHERN SIDE

This differs from the facade in decoration. The *Porta dei Fiori*, decorated in a quite sophisticated style, deserves special notice.

THE ATRIUM

The impact of this area is stunning thanks to the effect of the magnificent mosaic decoration, the sequence of marble colonnades, and the decorative elegance which gives it its overall and unforgettable appeal. The area is characterised by slightly pointed arches, resting on columns and interspersed with six small domes. The mosaic pavement is particularly fine; created in the twelfth century, it has geometric motives in repeating circular form.

A red stone placed under the second row of columns indicates the place where, according to tradition, the Emperor Frederick Barbarossa knelt before Pope Alexander III. The most significant work is the complex of *mosaics*, which completely cover the ceiling. These feature the *Stories of the Old Testament*, and of special interest are those of the first bay, the *Genesis Stories*, created in the first years of the thirteenth century. Also in the same bay is the *Door of San Clemente*, in bronze, with bas-reliefs portraying Saints, and remarkable capitals representing animals (which surmount the columns at the sides of the door). In the other bays and in the arcades, figures of *Apostles, Stories from the New Testament and figures of Saints* are added to the *Stories from the Old Testament*. Great artists from all epochs have worked on the mosaic designs. There are also a number of funerary monuments dedicated to some of the Doges of Venice. The right wing has been closed in to form the Baptistery and the Zen Chapel, which are entered from the interior of the church. The left wing of the Atrium opens at the far end through the splendid *Porta dei Fiori - the Floral Door*, decorated with elegant floral bas-reliefs.

INTERIOR

The sight of the interior can take the breath away. The overall effect of the gold of the mosaics, the interweaving of the architectural structures and the decoration which accompanies each element is unforgettable. Everything is harmonised in an atmosphere redolent of fairyland, and the gold and marble which cover every surface give mystery and grace to the severe rhythm of the arches and vaults. It has rightly been referred to as the *"Golden Basilica"* because gold is the dominant element in the decoration. It creates refractions, reflections, dazzling gleams which affect every part of the space, rendering it unreal and almost unlimited. We only need to remember that the mosaic cycle alone covers 4000 square metres, and that there are more than 500 columns. The plan of the building is a Greek cross with domes for each branch of the cross and a great central dome at the crossing. The floor, of variegated marbles, is made up of geometrical patterns. The lower section of the walls of the basilica is entirely covered with rare marble, and the columns which divide the church into naves are surmounted by fine capitals in bas-relief work.

THE CHAPELS AND PRESBYTERY:

LEFT TRANSEPT (A)

- Chapel of the Madonna dei Mascoli (1)
This takes its name from the Confraternity of the Mascoli (its members were exclusively male). It has a Gothic altar built by Giovanni Bon in the first years of the fifteenth century, crowned by marble statues. The mosaics are of particularly great interest here because they mingle the style of the Venetian school with that of the Renaissance. They portray *Stories in the Life of the Virgin Mary*, and were created on the basis of drawings by famous artists such as Andrea del Castagno, Giambono and Jacopo Bellini.

- Chapel of the Crucifix (2)
a complex of white and black columns surmounted by gilded capitals in the Byzantine style, which in turn hold up blocks of agate stone.

Mosaics of the Basilica, Doorway of Sant'Alipio: Translation of the Body of St Mark.

- **Holy Water Stoup** (3) - a Romanesque work of the twelfth century.
- **Doorway of the Madonna** (4)
- **Chapel of St Isidoro** (5): this was built in the fourteenth century on the orders of Doge Dandolo, to honour St Isidoro, whose remains were placed here in the sarcophagus of the main altar.

They had been transported to Venice in 1125. Magnificent mosaics of the 14th century decorate the chapel; they are among the most interesting in the Basilica because of the linear rhythm of the scenes represented and their narrative freshness. They tell *Stories of the life of St. Isidoro.*

- **Chapel of the Madonna of Nicopeia**

(6): so-called because of the venerated Byzantine image of the *Victorious Virgin*, transported to Venice by Doge Enrico Dandolo in the first years of the thirteenth century. It is a work of rare value, covered with gold and studded with precious stones. There is also a fine Renaissance altar.

- **The Altar of St Paul** (7): an elegant Renaissance work, carved by Pietro Lombardo and pupils of his school.
- **Double Pulpit** (8): so-called because it is made up of two pulpita, one above the other. Built in the fourteenth century, it consists of a lower part with an octagonal base and an upper one divided into sections and completed

Atrium of the Basilica of San Marco : this is formed by seven sections divided by arches. Both the floor and the upper part and dome are covered with mosaics.

INTERIOR OF THE BASILICA

A - LEFT TRANSEPT
B - PRESBYTERY
C - RIGHT TRANSEPT

1 - Chapel of the
    Madonna dei Mascoli
2 - Capital of the Crucifix
3 - Holy Water stoup
4 - Door of the Madonna
5 - Chapel of St Isidore
6 - Chapel of the
    Madonna di Nicopeia
7 - Altar of St Paul
8 - Double ambo
9 - Iconostasis
10 - Crypt of St Mark
11 - Chapel of St Peter
12 - Sacristy
13 - Ex Church of St Theodore
14 - Great Altar
15 - The Pala d' oro
16 - Chapel of St Clement
17 - Tabernacle of the Reliquaries
18 - Ambo of the Reliquaries
19 - Altar of the Sacrament
20 - Door
21 - Altar of St James
22 - Treasury
23 - Zen Chapel
24 - Baptistry

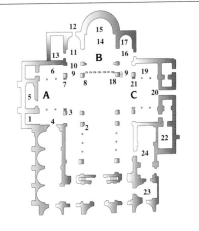

Mosaics of the Dome: Genesis - The Creation of Man.

Detail of the Mosaics in the Atrium: depiction of the Tower of Babel.

by columns supporting a small dome. The sculptures are works from the thirteenth century.

THE PRESBYTERY (B)

It stands over the crypt, and is separated from the rest of the Basilica by a large and magnificent iconostasis (9). This is a marble screen made up of a sequence of eight columns surmounted by capitals shimmering with gold, and by a row of statues (carved by Dalle Masegne), towards the end of the fourteenth century. It is a most exceptional example of Gothic art, and a masterpiece of Venetian sculpture.

-**The Crypt of San Marco** (10): it stands below the Presbytery, and contains the body of St Mark, patron of the city. It is divided into short naves with low columns and cross vaulting.

- **The Chapel of San Pietro** (11): has an iconostasis of marble statues made by the Dalle Massegne family. It is enriched by mosaics of the thirteenth century, a Gothic tabernacle, and a number of bas-reliefs.

- **The Sacristy** (12): a Renaissance room, decorated with mosaics based on designs by Titian and il Padovanino.

- **Former Church of San Teodoro** (13): once the Chapel of the Holy Office. Here one can see a work by Tiepolo, portraying the *Adoration of Jesus*. **High Altar**(14): in a richly decorated urn the body of St Mark is preserved here. Above four alabaster columns stands a ciborium, a thirteenth century work decorated with bas-reliefs figuring *Stories from the Gospels*. The bronze statues situated at the sides are by Jacopo Sansovino and Girolamo Paliari.

- **The Golden Altarpiece** (15): this is one of the most valuable works of the whole Basilica of San Marco. It is a huge work of gold craftsmanship, studded with precious stones. Made in the tenth century on the orders of Doge Orseolo by Byzantine and Venetian artists, it was completed and added to in the two subsequent centuries, then reassembled in its various parts by Gian Paolo Boninsegna, in 1345. The Golden Altarpiece spreads over a surface of about 3.5 metres (over 11 feet) in length, and the height is 1.4 metres (4.5 feet). It is made up of as many as 1300 pearls, hundreds of gems such as emeralds, sapphires, amethysts and rubies, and enamels and cameos.

- **The Chapel of San Clemente** (16):

Interior of the Basilica of San Marco: because of the splendour of its mosaics the church was called the "Golden Basilica".
The surfaces are entirely covered with mosaics.

characterised by an iconostasis in red marble, surmounted by statues carved by the Dalle Massegnes, representing the *Madonna and Child and other Saints*. The mosaics date from the twelfth century.

- **Tabernacle of the Relics** (17): This is an elegant Gothic structure and is decorated by statues and polychrome marbles.

- **The Ambo of the Reliquary** (18): A magnificent pulpit in rare marble, made in the fourteenth century but with parts coming from much more ancient Byzantine structures. It has a polygonal base resting on columns.

It was from this pulpit that the faithful were shown the relics. The decorations, featuring *peacocks* are Byzantine and date from the tenth century.

RIGHT WING OF THE TRANSEPT(C)

- **Altar of the Blessed Sacrament** (19): this was built of rare marbles in the seventeenth century. It holds the *Relics of the True Cross*. At the far end of this wing is the **Door** (20) which gives access to the Doges' Palace. There is a fine rose window placed above it, made even more elegant by decoration with small columns.

Basilica of San Marco: The Baptistry. The baptistry is decorated with fine mosaics (14th century) and a baptismal font by Sansovino whose tomb is also here.

- The Altar of San Giacomo (21): A Renaissance work dating from the mid-fifteenth century.

-The Treasury (22): Here a large number of precious objects have been gathered together, along with reliquaries of very high artistic merit. Some of them are masterpieces of the goldsmith's art.

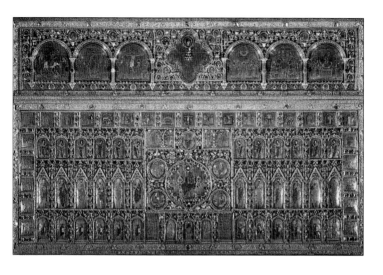

Basilica of San Marco: The "Golden Altarpiece".
The bronze horses of the Basilica.

The Zen Chapel (23):

This is the Chapel of Cardinal G.B.Zen, buried here in the fifteenth century (his burial monument is in the centre of the chapel). He had left his vast accumulated patrimony to Venice and to the Basilica. The statue of the *Madonna della Scarpa* carved by Antonio Lombardo in 1515 and placed on the altar is of high interest; it is so-called because there is a tradition which says that a simple cloth shoe left as an offering to the Madonna by a poor man was changed into gold.

The mosaics represent *The Madonna and Child* and *Christ and the Prophets* (end of the 13th century).

The Baptistery (24):

The area is divided into three parts. At the centre stands the *Baptismal Font*, carved in the sixteenth century by Sansovino. Around it are various tombs, among them that of Doge Andrea Dandolo (built by De Sanctis), who was the patron responsible for the decoration of the place. Among the mosaics, one the finest is above the altar portraying *Doge Dandolo adoring Christ on the Cross*. Other mosaics, mostly created in the mid-fourteenth century, recount *Stories of the Life of Christ, Stories of the Madonna,* and *Stories of St John Baptist*. In the Baptistery there is also the tomb of Jacopo Sansovino.

MOSAICS OF THE BASILICA

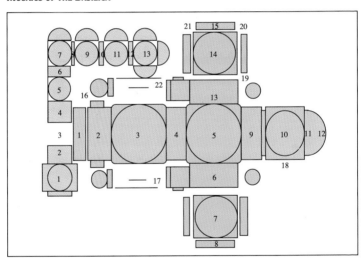

THE MOSAIC CYCLE

They almost entirely cover the walls of the Basilica, and form a complex of inestimable historical and artistic value. They cover more than 4000 square metres, and taken together they form a vast portrayal of the history of the Church.

Mosaics of the Atrium:

Old Testament Stories, Cain and Abel; The Stories of Noah, the Great Flood; The Apostles, Stories from the New Testament; The drunkenness of Noah; The Tower of Babel; Stories of Abraham; Justice; Stories of Joseph; Charity: Stories of Joseph; Saints; Stories of Joseph; Saints; Stories of Moses.

INTERIOR OF THE BASILICA

Mosaics of the upper part of the Church:

1 Arch of Paradise; the Church Triumphant, the Exaltation of the Cross; the Triumph of the Blessed; the Damnation of the Sinners (cartoons were by Tintoretto and Maffeo da Verona):

2 Arch of the Apoocalypse: Stories from the Apocalypse and visions of the end of the world.

3 Dome of Pentecost: The Preaching of the Apostles, and the Feast of Pentecost (a fine mosaic placed at the centre of the scene), The Conversion of the Multitudes.

4 Under the Arch: Stories of the Passion of Christ, a valuable thirteenth century mosaic, among the most interesting in the whole Basilica.

5 Dome of the Ascension: The Ascension of Christ among the Ängels and the Apostles (13th century).

6 Beneath the Arch: The Life of Christ, The Washing of Feet, The Last Supper, The Temptations of Christ, Entry to Jerusalem, the Eternal Father.

7 Dome of San Leonardo, or of the Blessed Sacrament: Saints (13th & 14th centuries).

8 Beneath the Arch of the Dome of San Leonardo: Miracles of Jesus. made in the 18th century, they surround a fine Gothic rose window.

9 Presbytery (beneath the arch): Stories of Jesus (drawings by Tintoretto).

10 Dome of the Presbytery: The Church as foreseen by the Prophets (12th to 13th centuries).

11 Beneath the Arch: The Lamb of God

12 Apse: Christ in the act of blessing, Prophets and Saints. This may be the oldest of all the mosaics.

13 Beneath the left Transept Arch: The Life of Christ and some miraculous episodes (cartoon designs by Tintoretto and Veronese).

14 Dome of San Giovanni Evangelista: Stories of Saint John the Evangelist (13th century).

15 Beneath the Transept Arch: Episodes in the life of Christ.

Mosaics in the lower part of the Church:

16 Christ blessing (13th century).

17 Saints (13th century mosaics): one of the most significant examples of the Venetian School.

18 Cain and Abel: Venetian art of the 12th century.

19 Chapel of the Madonna of Nicopeia: Madonna with Saints

20 Chapel of Sant'Isidoro: Episodes in the life of St.Isidoro, an amazing work of the fourteenth century.

21 Chapel of the Mascoli: Episodes in the Life of Mary, among the most outstanding works of the fifteenth century.

22 Prophets; 5 absolute masterpieces of Gothic art.

Other mosaics, to be found in the nave and the smaller domes, may be observed from the galleries of the Church.

From the Basilica, we go out into Piazza San Marco.

5.PROCURATIE VECCHIE OLD LAW COURTS

These were the meeting places of the "Procurators", or civil magistrates, of Venice, and their building was begun in the fifteenth century, by the architect Coducci. Their main feature is a long portico of 50 arches, surmounted by a double loggia of 100 arches.

6.PROCURATIE NUOVE NEW LAW COURTS

This building was constructed when it was decided to move the seat of the Procurators of San Marco from the old building. Designed by Vincenzo Scamozzi, it was completed by Baldassari Longhena at the beginning of the eighteenth century. Beneath the portico there is the famous Caffé Florian, the haunt of the cultural élite since the eighteenth century.

7. NAPOLEONIC WING

Also known as the New Building, it is characterised by 40 arches of two orders, built in 1807 on the area formerly occupied by the church of San Geminiano, in the same style, which dated from the end of the sixteenth century. The Correr Museum is situated in this building.

8. THE CORRER MUSEUM

The Museum takes its name from Teodoro Correr, an indefatigable collector or pictures, books, prints, precious objects and relics of antiquity found in the monasteries, churches and abandoned houses. The collection, of great value, was given to Venice in 1830. Subsequently the city itself added to it, thanks to numerous donations and to a series of purchases. This very variegated collection provides a kind of journey through the history and art of Venice. It is divided into sections:

1ST FLOOR

In the *Neo-classical Rooms* there is a collection of statues by A.Canova. This is followed by the *Historical collection* which, together with the *Collection of Renaissance Bronzes*, and that of the *Crafts, Trades and Games*, provides rich doumentation of the Republic of Venice. There are views of the city, by means of which it is possible to reconstruct its development over the years. Then there are banners, arrases, items of clothing with the famous "doges' cap", portraits of doges, paintings of historical episodes, coins, seals, arms of various types, nautical maps and also objects of Venetian craftsmanship, such as lace, majolica, bronzes and goldsmiths' work.

2ND FLOOR

Apart from the *Museum of the Risorgimento* which contains historical items relating to major episodes of the 19th century, this floor also contains the Art Gallery known as the *Quadreria*. The paintings are displayed according to period, beginning with the Byzantine age, which offers an overall view of the style of Venetian artists of the thirteenth and fourteenth centuries, and going on to the room of the most famous Venetian painters such as Lorenzo Veneziano, Vivarini, lo Schiavone, and Bellini, right through to the eighteenth century painter Pietro Longhi, famous for his *Views of the Lagoon*. Among the most important works we should mention those of Vivarini, represented by a *Madonna and Child* and a *St Anthony of Padua*. The works by Bellini are of major interest (a *Crucifixion* and a *Transfiguration*, masterpieces of the art of the late fifteenth century). Also worthy of note is the beautiful *Pietà* by Antonello da Messina, who worked in Venice in the second half of the fifteenth century, a *Crucifixion* by Ugo Van der Groes, and Carpaccio's famous painting of *Le Corteggiane*.

The *Gabinetto di Stampe e Disegni* (prints and drawings), and the *Ivory Collection* are also worth a visit.

9.THE PIAZZETTA, AND THE DOGES' PALACE

THE PIAZZETTA

The area included between the Basilica of San Marco and the Pier is known as the Piazzetta. On the one side it is enclosed by the Doges' Palace, and on the other by the Sansovino Library. The Basin of San Marco, which is immediately in front of the piazzetta, has been the main focal point of the city since the days of antiquity, and here all the most important buildings of the historic centre grew up. At the beginning of the Piazzetta there are two columns from the twelfth century, on the tops of which stand the statues of the Lion of St Mark and St Theodore.

10.THE LIBRARY

Built by Jacopo Sansovino in the middle of the sixteenth century, it was completed later by Vincenzo Scamozzi. There is a double loggiato with columns backed by pilasters, and surmounted by an elegant balustrade, and above the cornice by statues carved by a variety of artists. Inside, apart from the fine *Biblioteca Marciana*, there is also an Exhibition of

---

Panoramic view of Piazza San Marco and the buildings of the Procuratie Vecchie, the Procuratie Nuove and the Napoleonic Wing.

the Library's Treasures, a collection of pictorial and sculptural work which includes paintings by Tintoretto and Titian. The staircase which leads to the floor above is particularly fine, as is the Salone, a great hall of huge proportions, designed by Sansovino and decorated with paintings and sculptures. Delicate miniatures and codexes of incalculable value are stored in glass display-cases; among them the famous "Grimani Breviary", illuminated by Flemish artists. The Mappamondo di fra' Mauro deserves a special mention; a world-map designed in the sixteenth century, it provides a panorama of the continents known in that era, and their distribution over the earth's surface.

THE ARCHAEOLOGICAL MUSEUM

This is located behind the Sansovino Library. Formed at the end of the

sixteenth century, it is one of the oldest collections of its kind in existence. Of huge proportions, it has great importance for the knowledge of Greek and Roman sculpture. The Greek originals present are the most valuable part of the Museum: among these should be mentioned the Attic statue of A*thena, the* G*rimani* A*ltar,* and two works portraying a Gaul. There are also bronzes, ceramics, epigraphs, terracottas and vases, brooches and cameos, including a splendid Z*uleian* C*ameo* from the Hellenic Era. In addition there is a collection of archaeological finds from the excavations in the islands of Torcello, Malamocco and Eracle, which

Basilica of San Marco: The facade. The reflections of the sun enhance the beauty of the mosaics.

were among the first in the lagoon to be inhabited.

11.THE DOGES' PALACE

This is an extraordinarily beautiful building, and one which owes its uniqueness to the effect created by its decoration and overall architectural design. The elegant finesse of the loggias, the pinkish colour of the surfaces, further enhanced by delicate geometrical motifs, the richness of the filigree decoration which adorns the whole building, all add up to making this palace one of the highest and most original examples of late mediaeval architecture.

The Palace was the ancient residence of the Doges of Venice, and thus it was the centre of the city's life. The building took on its present form in the fifteenth century, but its origins are much earlier. In 814 there was already a building on its site, a fortress which underwent great transformations over the years, and was rebuilt in ways which meant that it more and more lost the original character of a castle and assumed that of an aristocratic and magnificent residence.

EXTERIOR

What strikes one first of all is the chromatic effect of the building. The white marbles of the loggiato and the pink and grey of the central facade create a startling effect, enhanced by the actual atmosphere, which is characteristic of Venice: the reflections of the water seem to play on the colours and the delicate motifs of the wall surfaces.

The palazzo has two facades, at right angles to each other; one looks out over the Basin of San Marco, while the other faces on to the piazzetta. The first is the older, and one can still see the balcony designed for it by Pier Paolo and Jacobello Dalle Masegne in 1404. Below runs a portico with sharply pointed arches, on low columns. Above this there is a loggiato, standing a little further back, and adorned between the arches with quatrefoil motifs. The upper section has a broad wall surface in multicoloured stone along which there are large windows at intervals. Further up again the top section is crowned with interlaced filigree work in white marble. There are three doors giving access to the interior of the Doges' Palace: the **Porta della Carta (A)**, which is the best known and opens on to Piazza San Marco, the **Porta del Frumento (B)** near the Pier, and the **Porta dell'Armar**, opening on to the Piazzetta and built in 1610.

THE PORTA DELLA CARTA (A)

This was the triumphal entrance to the Doges' Palace. It is so-called because it was near this doorway that the documents required by the citizens were on sale, and because the scribes had their desks here. It was built between 1438 and 1442 by the Bon brothers, and is a magnificent example of the flowering of Gothic architecture, with friezes, pinnacles and rich ornamentation.

INTERIOR

A visit to the Palace begins at the Porta del Frumento **(B)** through which access is obtained to the interior. As from June 1996, a new and more functional museum tour has been initiated, permitting the visitor to view the recent restorations and the new rooms opened to the public; in particular the **Museum of the Palace** works has been set up on the ground floor, and is of great historical and documentary interest. The *secret itineraries*, recently reorganised, and only visitable with special permission, reveal those parts of the palace which were more concerned with everyday life, and have remained outside traditional tourist visits.

GROUND FLOOR
FOSCARI COLONNADE
AND COURTYARD (C)

The enormous courtyard makes an immediate impact because of its elegance and ceremonial character, as well as by the mixture of architecture found there. It was built between the fifteenth and seventeenth centuries, and all the architectural styles from Gothic to late Renaissance are represented there. In the fifteenth century Antonio Rizzo worked there, and constructed the principal facade with its double loggia. In the middle of the 16th century it was the turn of Scarpagnino, while the decoration and polychrome marbles are attributed to Pietro Lombardo. The colonnade of the courtyard was built by Bon and completed by Bregno in the middle of the fifteenth century. The Arch of the Foscari **(c)** is directly in front of the Giants' Stairway.

General view of the buildings overlooking the Basin of San Marco. The Sansovinian Library can be seen on the left and the Doges' Palace on the right. In the background is the Basilica it self.

It is typically Venetian Gothic in style. Behind the Arch is the **Courtyard of the Senators (D)**.

The Lion of St Mark, statue surmounting the Porta della Carta.

In the centre of the space between the loggias are the two remarkable *bronze well-heads*, masterpieces by Alfonso Alberghetti and Niccolò dei Conti, mid 16th century.

THE GIANTS' STAIRCASE (E)

This is the name given to the grand entrance to the Palace. Built towards the end of the 15th century by Antonio Rizzo, the staircase provides access to the upper loggia. The stairway is decorated with huge marble statues carved by Sansovino, and it is these which give it its name.

Photo above: Doges' Palace: The Foscari Arch.
Photo below: Doges' Palace: the facade which looks towards the Basin of San Marco.

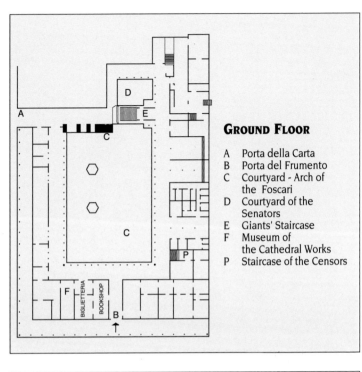

GROUND FLOOR

A   Porta della Carta
B   Porta del Frumento
C   Courtyard - Arch of
     the Foscari
D   Courtyard of the
     Senators
E   Giants' Staircase
F   Museum of
     the Cathedral Works
P   Staircase of the Censors

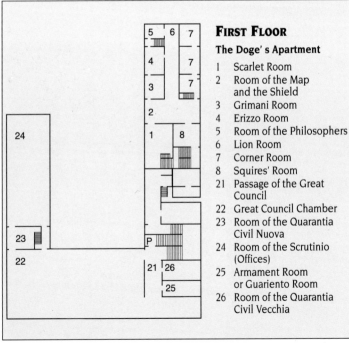

FIRST FLOOR

The Doge's Apartment

1   Scarlet Room
2   Room of the Map
    and the Shield
3   Grimani Room
4   Erizzo Room
5   Room of the Philosophers
6   Lion Room
7   Corner Room
8   Squires' Room
21 Passage of the Great
     Council
22 Great Council Chamber
23 Room of the Quarantia
     Civil Nuova
24 Room of the Scrutinio
     (Offices)
25 Armament Room
     or Guariento Room
26 Room of the Quarantia
     Civil Vecchia

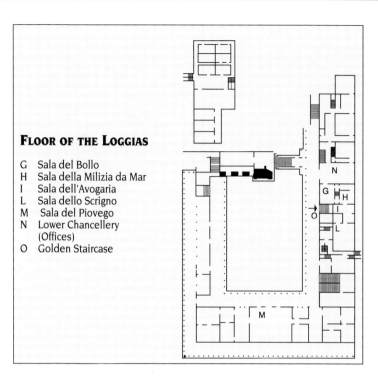

FLOOR OF THE LOGGIAS

G Sala del Bollo
H Sala della Milizia da Mar
I   Sala dell'Avogaria
L Sala dello Scrigno
M Sala del Piovego
N Lower Chancellery
    (Offices)
O Golden Staircase

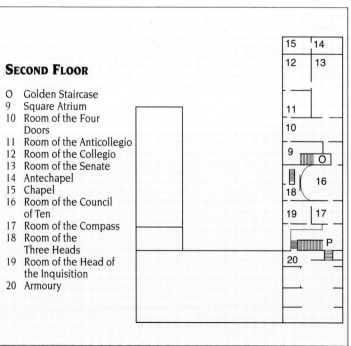

SECOND FLOOR

O   Golden Staircase
9   Square Atrium
10 Room of the Four
     Doors
11 Room of the Anticollegio
12 Room of the Collegio
13 Room of the Senate
14 Antechapel
15 Chapel
16 Room of the Council
     of Ten
17 Room of the Compass
18 Room of the
     Three Heads
19 Room of the Head of
     the Inquisition
20 Armoury

MUSUEM OF THE CATHEDRAL WORKS (F)

This is a group of rooms which have recently been set up: the materials on show have been distributed around the area which until the sixteenth century was the palace prison. Restoration work has revealed remains of the thirteenth century building.

The most interesting collection is that of the 32 original *capitals* - those of the colonnade and those of the loggia - which once graced the Doges' residence. Some of them, especially the thirteen which came from the colonnade, have biblical and allegorical subjects and date back to the fourteenth century; the others are mainly characterised by natural decoration, or by representations of historical and religious episodes. In the Museum, various other elements of the architecture of the Palace are also preserved.

THE FLOOR OF THE LOGGIAS

This is reached by the Staircase of the Censors (P). The loggias are distributed along the building and along the courtyard, right up to the *Foscari Loggia*, and they enhance the harmonic effect of the building. Among the rooms of this sector, we should mention the **Sala del Bollo, the Sala della Milizia da Mar (H), the Sala dell'Avogaria(I), and the Sala dell Scrigno (L).** The latter takes its name from the eighteenth century bureau which housed the lists of Venetian notables. Finally there are the **Sala del Plovego and the Lower Chancellery**: these were the offices of the Doges' administration.

THE GOLDEN STAIRCASE (O)

Planned by Sansovino, and completed by Scarpagnino, this formed the elegant entrance to the internal rooms of the Palace. It is embellished with gilded stucco work, which has given it the name by which it is known.

FIRST FLOOR
THE DOGE'S APARTMENT

1.The Scarlet Room. This takes its name from the scarlet colour of the robes worn by the Councillors who met here. It is an impressively elegant chamber, with delicate decoration by the Lombardo family, such as the *bas-relief of Doge Loredan* and the *Chimney-piece*. The gilded *wooden ceiling* is a masterpiece of the brothers Biagio and Pietro di Faenza.

2.Room of the Maps and the Shield: on the walls are displayed the great maps showing the world as then known, and the coat of arms of the Doge who was in office at that time.

3. Grimani Room: this has a fine fireplace by Lombardo.

4. Erizzo Room: has baroque decorations and a fireplace by Lombardo.

5. The Room of the Stuccos: a small chamber with very effective stucco decoration. From this room one passes out on to a terrace with a view over the Basilica of San Marco.

6. The Room of the Philosophers: on the walls are the portraits of the *Twelve Philosophers of Antiquity*. They were painted by Tintoretto and Veronese, and transferred here from the Library.

7. The Doge's Own Apartment (Lion Room, Corner Room and Portrait Room): This is a group of three chambers with works by Bellini (*The Lamentation of Christ*) and by Carpaccio (*a Lion*), and Bosch, represented here by one of his most important paintings of religious subjects.

On the staircase leading to the floor above is a *St.Christopher*, a famous fresco by Titian.

8. The Squires' Room (to the right of the staircase): here the great canvas by Titian is to be found, depicting *Venice receiving the homage of Neptune*. There are also works by Tintoretto and Palma the Younger.

SECOND FLOOR

9.The Square Atrium: served as an ante-chamber. It has a very fine ceiling with works by Tintoretto, portraying Doge *Girolamo Priuli*, and also by Veronese and Paolo Flammingo.

10. Room of the Four Doors: designed by Palladio, this room is so-called because four doors lead into it. The *ceiling* is painted by artists including Tintoretto, Tiepolo, Contarini and Titian, here represented by his portrait of *Doge Antonio Grimani*.

11. Room of the Anticollegio: a small chamber with frescos by Tintoretto, showing *mythological scenes*. It was rebuilt by Palladio and Vittoria after being destroyed by fire. Among the most important works, mention should be made of several masterpieces by Tintoretto (*Mercury and the Graces, Bacchus and Ariadne, Minerva and Mars*). The splendid *Rape of Europa* is by Paolo Veronese (late 16th century).

12. Room of the Collegio: This was the chamber used for the meetings of the Council. It is a very impressive room, and has a number of valuable artworks. The coffered ceiling is enriched by a masterpiece by Veronese, showing *Venus enthroned*, surrounded by symbolic representations of *the Virtues*. On the walls there are paintings with subjects from the *History of Venice*, together with portraits of a number of illustrious citizens.

Golden Staircase, Doges' Palace: *So-called because in the upper section it is covered with gilded plasterwork. It was designed by Sansovino and completed by Scarpagnino.*

Among the most famous paintings is one of the *Sacred Marriage of St Catherine* by Tintoretto.

13. Room of the Senate: this too was built after the disastrous fire of 1577. The walls and ceilings are completely covered with frescos by many artists, including Tintoretto, Palma the Younger and Antonio Vincentino, showing *Episodes in the History of Venice*.

14. The antechapel: a tiny area gracefully decorated with stucco work.

15. The Chapel: completely covered in frescos, it also has sculptures by Jacopo Sansovino, including a *Madonna and Child* (on the altar).

From here we return to the Room of the Four Doors (10) and pass on to:

16. The Room of the Council of Ten: copies of paintings by Paolo Veronese depicting mythological scenes are inserted into the wooden inlay ceiling.

17. Room of the Compass: this served as an antechamber to the Room of the Council of Ten. It has a fine fireplace by Sansovino, and several paintings.

18. Room of the Three Heads of the Council of Ten: (this is part of the "Secret Tour"): the ceiling is decorated by various artists, including Veronese.

19. Room of the Head of the Inquisition: (part of the "Secret Tour"): linked to the Bridge of Sighs by a secret passage, and to the Torture Chamber, it has a ceiling painted by Tintoretto.

20 The Armoury: or Room of the Weapons: it has on display a varied and interesting collection of weapons. These have always been kept in these rooms because they were used by the Councillors themselves for their own defence. Among the rarest pieces is a 'colubrina' of the 16th century, the armour once thought to belong to Gattamelata, and that of King Henri IV of France.

FIRST FLOOR

We return to the First Floor by way of the Scala dei Censori (P):

21. Passage of the Great Council:. a passageway between the Room of the Council of Ten and the remain-

---

Doges' Palace: Room of the Four Doors. Designed by Palladio, it has a ceiling painted by Tintoretto.

Room of the Anticollegio.

der of the Building.

22. Great Council Chamber: the proportions are vast, and the blend of architecture and decoration is sumptuous. Here the 'Nobili' of Venice, inscribed in the Golden Book, used to meet. The chamber was painted with frescos by Guariento, and then, after the fire which devastated it, by the greatest artists of the City, including Bellini, Carpaccio, Veronese and Tintoretto.

The paintings:

a) *Paradise* by Tintoretto: a work of vast dimensions (7 metres by 22), especially interesting in the complexity of its composition, the play of light and shade and the extraordinary number of persons represented. It was painted with the help of many assistants, because the master himself by this time was quite old.

b) *Episodes in the life of Doge Sebastiano Ziani, Pope Alexander III and Frederick I Barbarossa.*

c) *Episodes in the story of Venice.*

d) Representation of the *Fourth Crusade*, and Venice's participation in this event.

On the ceiling are works by Veronese, portraying the *Apotheosis of Venice*, another of the painter's great masterpieces. The arrangement of the figures is especially striking, as is the attention paid to architectonic detail and the overall decorative taste of the work.

23. The Room of the Quarantia Civil Nuova (New Civil Court): this was the Court of appeal for civil cases.

Above: Doges' Palace: Room of the Collegio: this is one of the most sumptuous rooms of the Palace, and has masterpieces by several great artists. Among these, special mention should be made of the Battle of Lepanto by Veronese.

Above to the right: Doges' Palace: Hall of the Maggior Consiglio. The largest of the halls in the Palace.

There are many paintings including Tintoretto's Paradise.

It was repainted after the sixteenth century fire, by Bellini, Carpaccio, Veronese and Tintoretto.

To the right: Doges' Palace: Senate Hall. This room, where the Senators of the Republic met, is solemn and richly decorated in character.

Room of the Three Heads of the Council of Ten.

The room has 16th century decoration.

24. The Room of the Scrutinio (Election of the Doge): it possesses a *Triumphal Arch* in imitation of those of the Roman era. The paintings are by imitators of Tintoretto and Veronese. On the wall directly in front of the arch is the *Last Judgment* by Palma the Younger. The *Battle of Lepanto* was painted by Vicentino.

25. Armament Room or Guariento Room: it takes its name from the fresco by Guariento, illustrating *Paradise* (14th century). Recently restored, the painting beautifully depicts *The Coronation of the Virgin*.

26. Room of the Quarantia Vecchia (Old Court): this has decorations from the seventeenth century. It was the old Appeal Court.

PRISONS

We come next to the ancient and sadly notorious prisons of Venice. The part which was underground was known as *"Piombi"* (the leads) because the walls were lined with strips of lead, which made them broiling and unbearable in the summer heat. The prisons which were above ground, on the other hand, were known as *"Pozzi"* (the wells) because they were subject to flooding for many days of the year, and even when this was not the case they were extremely humid.

Casanova was imprisoned in the Piombi, and was involved in a wildly adventurous flight, described by him in his *Memoirs*.

12. THE BRIDGE OF SIGHS

The architecture is delicate and original in style; it was built in 1589 by Antonio Contin, and is one of the most famous bridges in the world.

It was built to link the Court to the Prisons. It was known as the Bridge of Sighs because of the moans of the condemned when, after receiving their sentence, they crossed the brief tract which separated them from their cells, and saw the light of day for the last time.

Bridge of Sighs.

THE GRAND CANAL

The Grand Canal is the main artery of Venice, and together with Piazza San Marco and the Doges' Palace, it forms the greatest attraction of the city. Because of the exceptional beauty of the buildings which face on to it and the fascination arising from the slow revelation of fine and elegant architecture which is reflected in the water; because of the strange and evocative jostling of gondolas and *vaporetti*, it provides an itinerary of unequalled interest, a fascinating passage through the centuries of the economic and political and artistic history of this unique place.

The effect created by the interlacing of the tracery decorating the palaces reflected in the Grand Canal is unforgettable, and adds even more to the unrivalled appeal of the whole. The waters reflect delicate, elaborate architectural decorations; they repeat the chromatic effects of the wall-surfaces, and add even more facets to them. In this way an atmosphere of fable is created, an unreal world which provokes profound reactions at every turn.

The Grand Canal winds along for almost four kilometres, drawing a great S back to front through the heart of the historical centre, and linking Piazzale Roma to the Bay of San Marco and the Doges' Palace.

Historically it is the nucleus of the development of the Venetian Republic. Here the goods from the East arrived, to be deposited in the ancient warehouses which stood in large numbers on the banks of the Canals. And here were the mansions of the city's aristocracy, and the richest merchants.

These amazing buildings, which are the characteristic element of the Grand Canal, bear excep-

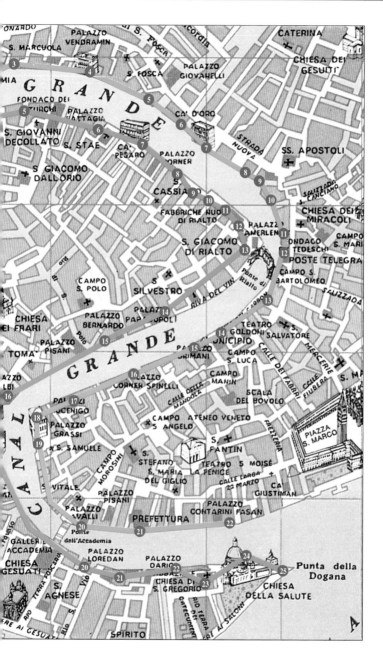

tional witness to an architectural history ranging from the Romanesque to the Baroque.

Piazzale Roma

This is the nerve-centre of the traffic coming from the land. Here the buses, trains and cars from the mainland arrive and discharge. The area is well-provided with garages and services.

THE LEFT BANK

1. Pontile (Wharf) of Santa Lucia: Railway station and departure point for the vaporetti.

Ponte degli Scalzi (Friars' Bridge): this is the first of the three bridges which cross the Grand Canal. It was built in 1934, to a design by Eugenio Miozzi.

2.Church of the Scalzi (Shoeless Friars). A baroque building with a facade by Giuseppe Sardi and an interior by Longhena (see Itinerary 5).

3. Palazzo Correr Contarini or Ca' dei Cuori (17th century). Characterised by two loggias, one above the other, standing out from the rose-coloured surface of the plasterwork.

4. Palazzo Vendramin Calergi: a magnificent building erected in the first years of the 16th century by Mauro Coducci and the Lombardos. The facade is in an elegant Renaissance style, reinterpreted according to the quite distinctive taste of Venetian architecture, with fine two-light windows creating a double-loggia. It was here that the musician Richard Wagner died. It is now the winter-home of the gambling casino.

5. Palazzo Gussoni-Grimani della Vida: an elegant Renaissance building with rustication below and two windowed loggias above.

6.Palazzo Fontana: sixteenth century construction which was the birthplace of Carlo Rezzonico.

7.Ca' d'Oro: This is one of Venice's most facinating monuments. The splendid palace is one of the finest examples of late-flowering Gothic. It was built in the first years of the 15th century. Half the palace is characterised by three loggiatas, one above the other, with interwoven arches and exquisitely carved tracery. In the right half of the front side, there are delicate windows resting on balconies with elegant balustrades. The building is further enriched by polychrome underscor-

THE RIGHT BANK

1. The Papadopoli Garden: a green space, small in dimensions but with its own charm and grace.

2. Palazzi Diedo (18th century), in the neo-classical style, with a fine colonnade.

3. Church of San Simeone Piccolo (see Itinerary 3). The Church, which originated in the 800s, was completely rebuilt in the 18th century in neoclassical style. It is somewhat reminiscent of the Pantheon. The copper-covered dome, which has taken on a particular patina, is particularly fine. The church now serves as an auditorium.

The decorations which once adorned the facade have long since disappeared; they were attributed to artists such as Giorgione and Titian.

4. Casa Correr: this was the first nucleus of the Correr Museum.

5. Fondaco dei Turchi: a building constructed in the 12th and 13th centuries. This is a magnificent structure, Byzantine in lines but modified according to the Venetian style. Historically speaking, it is one of Venice's most significant buildings as well as one of its oldest. Characterised by an elegant and airy portico, above which a loggia stands, it is crowned with crenellated work. The *Museum of Natural History* (see Itinerary No.3) is housed here.

6. The Church of San Stae: an eighteenth century building in the baroque style (see Itinerary 3).

7. Palazzo Pesaro: one of the most important buildings by Longhena, later completed by Gaspari. It houses the *National Art Gallery.* (see Itinerary 3).

The lower part of the building has very pronounced rustication; the two upper storeys are made up of two loggias with architraves, and have rows of single and grouped columns.

THE LEFT BANK

ing. At one time the surfaces were all gilded, hence the name given to the palace, and this must have conferred a truly exceptional appearance on the whole building. This is where the Galleria Franchetti is housed. (see Itinerary 5).

8. Palazzo Michiel dalle Colonne and **Michiel dal Brusà**: the first dating from the seventeenth century and the second from the eighteenth. Brusà is the local way of saying "bruciato", i.e. burnt; the building was in fact once destroyed by a fire.

9. Palazzo Mangilli-Valmarana: this is in the neoclassical style of the late 18th century.

10. Ca'Da Mosto: an elegant building in the Veneto-Byzantine style. Although much restored, it still remains very elegant in appearance and decoration. It was the birthplace of Alvise Da Mosto, the man who discovered Cape Verde Island.

11. Campiello del Remer is one of the most picturesque corners of Venice.

12. Fondaco dei Tedeschi: the archiect was Scarpagnino, and the building is in Renaissance style. On the lower floor there is a spacious loggia.

13. Palazzo Manin: again Renaissance in style, with a wide portico on the lower floor.

14. Palazzo Loredan: this is now the seat of the City Council. The building dates from the thirteenth century.

15. Palazzo Grimani: the home of the Appeal Court, it was built in the 16th century by Sammichele. The fine building has three loggias one above the other, in harmonious unity.

16. Palazzo Corner-Spinelli: the building is made up of a lower section in rusticated style and an upper one with twin-lancet windows. It is a masterpiece of 15th and 16th century architecture.

17. Palazzo Mocenigo: a complex constructed in the 16th and 17th

THE RIGHT BANK

8. Palazzo Corner della Regina: an eighteenth century building built over a previous one which belonged to Caterina Cornaro, Queen of Cyprus.

9. Palazzo Favretto: previously belonged to the Bragadin family (16th century).

10. Pescheria (Fishmarket): This was built in 1907 in imitation of the typical style of Venetian buildings facing on to the Grand Canal. The building, which is in red plasterwork, has an airy loggia on the lower floor - which is where the fish market is actually held - and a narrower one on the floor above.

11. New Buildings of the Rialto: built by Sansovino in the 16th century, today they are the home of the Judicial Court and Offices.

12. Old Buildings of the Rialto: this is also a sixteenth century building, this time by Scarpagnino. It has rows of rectangular windows on both floors. In the square in front of it, the main market is held.

Rialto Bridge.

This is one of the most typical and symbolic monuments of Venice, and one of the most justly famous all over the world. 50 (160 feet) metres long, it is built in the form of one great arch, above which, on both sides, runs a loggia which is raised to a greater height in the centre. It was built at the end of the sixteenth century by Antonio Da Ponte.

Previously there were other bridges in this stretch of the Canal. The first, a simple group of pontoons, dated from 1180; in the mid thirteenth century, it was replaced by another in wood. This fell down in 1444, and in its place yet another wooden bridge was built, which lasted until the construction of the present one.

13. Palazzo dei Camerlenghi (Chamberlains): elegant and sober Renaissance building.

THE LEFT BANK

centuries, with several buildings behind a single facade. The *Centre for the Study of Textiles and Costume* is housed here.

18. Palazzo Contarini delle Figure: a Renaissance style building.

19. Palazzo Grassi: A stylistically very well-balanced building, with elegant architectural forms. It was built in the 18th century and the project was carried out by Giorgio Massari. It houses the *Centre for the Arts and Costume*, and each year important exhibitions, collections, conferences and cultural events are held here. Some of the exhibitions linked to the Biennale are kept in its rooms.

The Ponte dell'Accademia: this is the third of the bridges over the Grand Canal. It is a wooden bridge and has a singe great arch. It takes its name from the Gallery of the Academy which stands in a nearby square.

20. Palazzo Cavalli Franchetti: in Gothic style, but rebuilt towards the end of the nineteenth century.

21. Palazzo Corner or Ca'Grande: The designer was Sansovino. On the lower floor there are three great arches, while in the two upper floors there are two orders of windows divided up by semi-columns.

22. Palazzo Contarini-Fasan: this dates from the second half of the fifteenth century, and is in the typical Venetian Gothic style.

THE RIGHT BANK

14. Palazzo Papadopoli: another Renaissance building, with a very harmonious architectural structure. The two obelisks standing on the roof are original. Inside there are paintings by Tiepolo; it also has an interesting hall of mirrors.

15. Palazzo Bernardo: fifteenth century building in the Gothic style, characterised by a series of delicate and richly decorated arches.

16. Palazzo Balbi: also known as the "Canal Vault" because it is perched on the curve of the Canal. Its architecture is late Renaissance.

17. Ca' Foscari: This is one of the most beautiful examples of later flowering Gothic. The brick-coloured facade is lightened by the delicate crenellation of the marble loggias with their finely decorated windows. It was built in the fifteenth century.

18. Palazzo Giustinian: this is in fact a combination of two palazzi from the fifteenth century, with finely decorated windows.

19. Ca' Rezzonico: The building was begun by Longhena, in the second half of the seventeenth century, but it was not completed (by Massari) until the 1700s. The construction is based on three orders of loggias divided by balustrades, and given movemnt by a series of columns. Here the *Museum of the Venetian Eighteenth century* has its home (see Itinerary 3).

20. Palazzo Barbarigo: a fine palace of the nineteenth century, the facade of which is decorated in theatrical manner with mosaics of historical subjects by Giulio Carlini.

21. Palazzo Venier dei Leoni: in this building the prestigious Peggy Guggenheim Collection of contemporary art is housed. (see Itinerary 3.)

22. Palazzo Dario: This has an original facade built by Pietro Lombardo in 1487. The left hand side has a

THE RIGHT BANK

series of loggias, while in the central part, where rose-coloured marbles predominate, there are finely decorated traceried windows.

23. The Abbey of San Gregorio: (see Itinerary 3).

24. Church of Santa Maria della Salute: a splendid building by Baldassare Longhena. (see Itinerary 3).

25. Dogana da Mar (Customs House): seventeenth century building which stands at the far end of the Grand Canal (se Itinerary 3). The Grand Canal ends at the Bay of San Marco, the magnificent civil and religious heart of the city of Venice.

Above: *View over the Rio.*
Centre: *Church of the Scalzi.*
Below: *Palazzo Vendramin Calergi.*

On this page:
Ca' Pesaro: here
the National Art
Gallery is housed.

Palazzo Corner
della Regina
(18th century).

Overleaf: *Fondaco
dei Turchi
(12th-13th
centuries).
The architecture
is in the
Byzantine style.
It houses the
Museum of
Natural History.*

Ca' d'Oro: one of
the most admired
and richly ornate
of Venice.
Inside, is the
Franchetti
Gallery.

View over the Grand Canal and the Pescheria.
Below: Rialto Bridge. Following page - above: Palazzo Grassi, built in the 18th century. It houses the Centre for Art and Costume.

THE HISTORICAL REGATTA

The Regatta is the most typical and fascinating festival in Venice. It recalls the years when the city was Mistress of the Marine Republics.

A procession of boats parades down the Grand Canal carrying rowers and historical personalities in period costumes. Most splendid of all is the Bucintoro, the boat used by the Doges.

THE CARNIVAL OF VENICE

A rich, sumptuous and joyous Venetian event. For days on end Venetians wearing the most beautiful and typical fancy-dress costumes parade through the city.

FESTIVAL OF THE "REDENTORE"

The festival was introduced as a thanksgiving to the Redeemer (Redentore) for the end of a plague epidemic in 1576. Today it is one of the most moving and theatrical events in the Venetian calendar. Together with religious ceremonies and the procession, a number of spectacles and festivities are held; especially the splendid procession of boats hung with lights and decorations.

Images of the Historical Regatta on the Grand Canal.
Overleaf, below: *Feast of the Redeemer.*

Palazzo Corner, or Ca'Grande:
below: Palazzo Cavalli Franchetti, a building restored in Gothic style in the 1900s.
Overleaf, above: Ca'Foscari: the building dates from the first years of the fifteenth century and is one of the finest examples of late-flowering Gothic.
Centre: Ponte dell'Accademia: one of the three bridges across the Grand Canal. It is made of wood and has a wide large arch.
Below: Palazzo Venier dei Leoni: this is the home of the valuable Art Collection of Peggy Guggenheim, one of the most prestigious collections of modern art in the world.

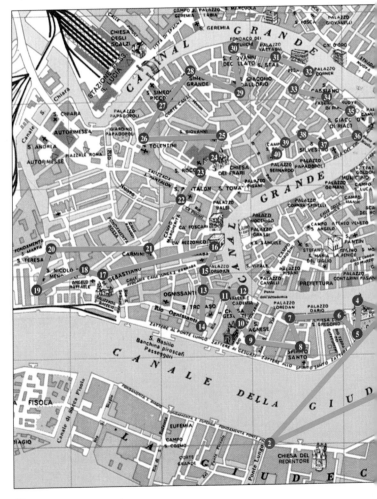

1. THE ISLAND OF SAN GIORGIO

In the past this island was known as the "Isle of Cypresses" because it had a considerable area of greenery. At the end of the tenth century, on the orders of Doge Morosini, a monastery was built here. Since 1951, the Giorgio Cini Foundation has had its headquarters in this monastery; a foundation which has played a great international role in the spread of culture and in the presentation of art exhibitions of the highest level. Its activity is mainly in the study of Venetian civilisation, in the field of literature - the Library in the Foundation is one of the richest in Italy - and in art, music and theatre.

THE CHURCH OF SAN GIORGIO MAGGIORE

This is a magnificent Palladian building: the white facade flanked by the tall, imposing tower dominates the southern side of the Bay of San Marco. Begun in the sixteenth century on the foundations of an older church dating back to the eleventh, it was completed in 1610.
It has four large columns forming a single order. Above these is a timpanum, while beside them are the two wings corresponding to the two lateral naves inside the church. Between the columns are the main entrance, and two niches with statues of St George and St Lawrence.

53

The *interior* is stately and harmonious, in the form of a basilica. It is adorned with works by Bassano and Tintoretto, represented here by his masterpiece portraying *The Last Supper*, and by the so-called *Gathering of the Manna*. Another fine work is the *St.George killing the Dragon* by Carpaccio.

A work of great originality is the sixteenth century wooden choir.

The ascent of the tower is a great delight; from it an unforgettable view over the whole city can be obtained.

2. THE GIUDECCA ISLAND

The island lies at the southern end of Venice, along the Giudecca Canal (1600 metres in length), the main commercial artery of Venice.

It is in fact made up of a group of 8 islets, linked by a long street called the Fondamenta.

The environment of the Giudecca is a most interesting urban architectural complex, for it unites in itself popular houses, noble mansions, open spaces and silent little lanes.

CHURCH OF THE ZITELLE (SPINSTERS) OR OF SANTA MARIA DELLA PRESENTAZIONE

This has a classical-style facade by Palladio, with a timpanum, an octagonal plan and a large dome. The interior, of eighteenth century design, has works by Palma the Younger, Bassano and Vassilacchi.

CHURCH OF THE REDENTORE (REDEEMER)

The magnificent architecture is by Palladio and Antonio da Ponte. It was erected in the mid-sixteenth century as a thankoffering to the redeemer for the end of the plague which had afflicted Venice in 1576. The classical facade rises above a wide staircase, and has a grand doorway flanked by two rows of pilasters.

Church of San Giorgio Maggiore, built by Palladio. In the interior there are works by Tintoretto and Carpaccio. On the island, in the buildings of the Monastery, the Fondazione Giorgio Cini has its headquarters. The Foundation is particularly famous for its cultural activities.

The interior is in the form of a Latin cross, and attracts the attention of the visitor by its overall elegance and the measured balance of the architectural design.

There are many paintings and sculptures in the church: to mention a few, the *Flagellation of Christ* (Tintoretto and his pupils); the *Baptism of Christ* probably by Veronese, and paintingns by Bassano and Vivarini.

CHURCH OF SANT'EUPHEMIA

A building of ancient origins which has been much restored. The decoration of the interior is mainly eighteenth century; the capitals, however, come from the Venetian-Byzantine period.

3. PUNTA DELLA DOGANA

This is the far point of the Grand Canal, facing on to the Bay of San Marco. The seventeenth century building is characterised by a turret and a great statue of Fortune, resting on a globe which turns in harmony with the statue.

4. THE CHURCH OF THE SALUTE

This exceptional church, with its delicate and articulated architecture, dominates the scene at the end of the Grand Canal. Building began in 1630, as a thankoffering to the Madonna who was believed to have brought an end to the terrible outbreak of plague. It was designed by Baldassare Longhena, who produced a real masterpiece of baroque art.

The plan is octagonal, divided into a series of projecting sections, the largest of which acts as a facade. Opposite this is a broad and lightly designed stairway. The main body of the building is surmounted by an open drum with tall, deep-set windows. Above this rises the majestic and dignified dome, culminating in a lantern. Broad volutes link the the

lower section to the upper part. Each element of the building is enriched with statues, cornices and bas-reliefs, so that the overall effect is of great richness. A second smaller dome placed above the presbytery, and two small campaniles complete the overall scheme.

The interior is almost theatrical in effect, for the octagonal plan, the breadth of the central area, the movement bestowed by the columns and chapels, create an atmosphere of solemn grandeur.

In the Presbytery there is the High Altar, surmounted by a marble reredos figuring the *Plague fleeing before the Virgin*. This contains the venerated image of the *Madonna della Salute*, a Byzantine icon brought to Venice by Francesco Morosini in 1672.

The wooden choir dates from the sixteenth century.

Among the other works we should mention the **Sacristy**: the great painting by Tintoretto portraying the *Marriage in Cana* is surely one of the artist's finest works. There are also paintings by Titian, among them those featuring *Old Testament Stories* and in particular *The Sacrifice of Abraham* and *David and Goliath*.

Church "Della Salute".

5. PATRIARCHAL SEMINARY

The seventeenth century building contains an exhibition of pictures and sculpture. In the Cloister there is a collection of memorial stones and tombstones.

in the **Manfrediana Picture Gallery** (which takes its name from its former propritor, Count Marchesini), there are paintings by Filippo Lippi, Antonio Vivarini, Titian, Veronese, and Cima da Conegliano. We should also mention some of the busts, the terracottas of Alessandro Vittoria, and one by Canova. There are also interesting statues by Benedetto Antelami (13th century) and bas-reliefs by Pietro Lombardo, as well as a number of Gothic panels.

6. FORMER ABBEY AND CHURCH OF SAN GREGORIO

The twelfth century abbey formed an integral whole with the nearby ninth century church. The Gothic facade of the church with its two-lancet windows and pilasters dividing the surface is unusual and striking.

The Abbey cloister is beautiful, as is the facade with its Gothic rosette windows and a niche with a statue of St.Gregory.

7. PALAZZO VENIER DEI LEONI - PEGGY GUGGENHEIM ART COLLECTION

This is one of the most important collections of contemporary art in the world, and certainly the richest and most valuable in Italy. The collection takes its name from its founder and patron Peggy Guggenheim, who owned the Palazzo.

The most important artists in the areas of cubism, futurism, dadaism, surrealism and abstractism are all represented here; there are many masterpieces by Picasso, Braque, Boccioni, Kandinksy, Mondrian, Chagall, Max Ernst, Pollock, Vedova, Pomodoro, Duchamp, De Chirico, Severini, Marcoussis, Magritte, Paul Klee and Mirò.

8. CHURCH OF SANTO SPIRITO

This was built towards the end of the 15th century, in Renaissance style. In the interior, refurbished in the seventeenth and eighteenth centuries, there is a monument by Longhena dedicated to the Paruta family, and several paintings, including those of Palma the Younger.

9. CHURCH OF SANT'AGNESE

Only the central part of the original building remains as the rest was mostly destroyed by a fire.

10. CHURCH OF THE GESUATI

Also known as Santa Maria del Rosario, it was built in classical style by Giorgio Massari in the first part of the 18th century. The interior, with a single nave, is particularly fine. A row of columns backs on to the walls. The sculptures and paintings are of special interest:
- Right wall:
1st altar: *Madonna and Child and Saints*, a lovely work by Giovan Battista Tiepolo.
2nd altar: *St.Dominic* by Piazzetta
3rd altar: *St Vincent Ferraris and Saints* by Piazzetta.
- Presbytery:
frescos by Tiepolo on the ceiling. 18th century wooden choirstalls.
- Left wall:
3rd altar: *Crucifixion* - a beautiful work by Tintoretto.
2nd altar: *Madonna with a rosary* by Antonio Bosa;
1st altar: *Saints* by Sebastiano Ricci.

11. CHURCH OF SANTA MARIA DELLA VISITAZIONE

This is a fifteenth century church, with a fine Renaissance facade. In the interior there are several works of the Umbrian school, painted by Agabiti.

Above: The Accademia delle Arti. This houses the Gallery of the Academy where there are works of artists from the 14th to the 18th centuries.
Below: Vittorio Carpaccio: The Dream of St Ursula, an episode taken from the Stories of St Ursula.

Above: *Gallery of the Academy*: "St. Mark saving a Saracen" - Tintoretto.
Below: *Gallery of the Academy*: Healing of a possessed man, by Vittore Carpaccio.

Gallery of the Academy: Miracles of the Cross, by Gentile Bellini.

A convent stands beside the church, and it is possible to visit the attractive cloister.

12. GALLERY OF THE ACCADEMIA

This is a big museum complex housing works of great historical and artistic value, ranging from the fourteenth to the eighteenth centuries.

They provide a broad spectrum of Venetian painting and its evolution over the centuries. The historical nucleus of the Gallery comes from the group of paintings collected for study by the Academicians. Subsequently, it was enriched by numerous bequests, and also by a series of important purchases.

It was opened to the public from 1817 onwards, and is now housed in a whole group of buildings, including the Great School, the Church of Santa Maria della Carità (15th century), and the Monastery of the (Augustinian) Canons.

The collection, distributed throughout 24 rooms, tells the story of five centuries of Venetian painting, and some of the very finest works of the artists represented are on display. There are a large number of paintings by Giovanni Bellini (known as Il Giambellino), one of the greatest exponents of Venetian painting in the late fifteenth century, and the man who brought renewal to it. He was able to give the plastic quality and sense of volume peculiar to Renaissance art to his scenes and figures, but he modified the effect by his softness of line, and above all by his use of luminous, soffused colours. Among the paintings in the Gallery, we would mention especially:

- *Sacra Conversazione,* or *The Altarpice of San Giobbe*;
- *Madonna and Child and Saints Catherine and Mary Magdalene*;
- *Le Allegorie*: five small works forming part of the decoration of a piece of furniture;
- *Madonna and Child*, known as the *Madonna of the Little trees*;
- *La Pietà*: possibly the most famous and expressive of the artist's works.
- *Head of the Redeemer*
- *Triptych of St.Lawrence*;
- *Triptych of the Madonna*
- *Triptych of St Sebastian*;
- *Triptych of the Nativity.*

Also worthy of note is the *Procession in Piazza San Marco* by Gentile Bellini, a work of exceptional expressive power.

Gallery of the Academy: Paolo Veronese - The Supper in the House of Levi, the figures are exceptional, as is the richness of detail which characterises the scene.
Gallery of the Academy: Giorgione - La Tempesta , one of the most famous paintings of this artist, and a masterpiece of 16th century Italian art.

61

Ca' Rezzonico: An 18th century building by Longhena. It houses the interesting Museum of 18th century Venice.

The Venetian painting of Byzantine inspiration (14th century) is of special interest. Paolo, Lorenzo and Caterino Veneziano are all represented (*The Coronation of the Virgin* and *The Annunciation and Four Saints*, together with Jacobello da Fiore, with his *Coronation of Mary.*

Giorgione is represented by some of his most important paintings; justly famous is *La Tempesta* which arrests the attention because of the innovative way in which landscape is used and the remarkable use of colour. An original and exeptionally expressive painting is the portrait of *An Old Woman* by the same painter.

The very beautiful *Stories of Saint Ursula* is one of the outstanding works by Carpaccio, while among the Titians, there is the *St John Baptist*, and the amazing *Pietà*, the artist's last work - full of dramatic expression and suffused with the agonised distortion of the forms.

Veronese is represented by his masterpiece, *The Supper in the House of Levi*. Painted in 1573, it provides a spectacular representation, in great detail, of the costumes and the architecture of Venice in that period.

There are many Tintorettos in the collection: *The Miracle of St Mark* is possibly the most important. This is made up of two canvasses, in which he stresses the dynamism of the figures, and above all the use of chiaroscuro to render the expressive quality of the scene more vivid. Other paintings by the same artist include *Adam and Eve*, *The Presentation of Christ in the Temple*; *Cain and Abel* and *The Deposition from the Cross*.

The Gallery also displays works by Mategna (*St George*), Cosmè Tura (a *Madonna and Child*), Piero della Francesca (*St Jerome*), Lorenzo Lotto (*Portrait of a Gentleman*), Paris Bordone (*The Giving of the Ring*) and Palma the Elder (*Sacra Conversazione*).

Ca' Rezzonico: this is a faithful and valuable reconstruction of a Venetian house inhabited by a noble family. There are contemporary furnishings, hangings, paintings and tapestries, and works of various types form this period in the history of the city.

We can also find paintings by Basaiti, Benedetto Diana, Vivarini, Sebastiano del Piombo, Pordenone and Schiavone.

13. CHURCH OF SAN TROVASO

Built in the 16th century on the site of a more ancient church, it has fine Renaissance lines. The facade is broken up by pilasters, with a wide doorway and a large lunette in the upper section. The interior is in the form of a single nave, with lateral chapels. There are many works of art, including the splendid painting by Jacobello da Fiore, portraying *St Crisogono*. Titian and Tintoretto are also represented, and among the sculptures, there is the bas-relief by

Pietro Lombardo, the subject of which is *The Symbols of the Passion*.

14. SQUERO DI SAN TROVASO

A s*quero* is a small dockyard, and this is probably the oldest, and certainly the most typical of those in Venice. Built in the 17th century to build and repair boats, and so above all, the characteristic Venetian gondola, it has kept its character virtually unchanged. The houses, mainly in wood and brick, face on to the quays, which are also made of wood, and provide a glimpse of a past which has remained unchanged.

15. CHURCH OF SAN BARNABA

An eighteenth century building designed by Boschetti. The facade is made up of a single order of four great columns. Beside it stands a robust-looking brick bell-tower of the fourteenth century.

The interior, with a single nave flanked by columns, is decorated in the 18th century style.

16. THE CA' REZZONICO AND THE MUSEUM OF THE VENETIAN EIGHTEENTH CENTURY

The palace was begun by Longhena in the seventeenth century and completed by Massari in the eighteenth. The rooms, splendidly decorated by Tiepolo and other artists, have housed the Museum of Eighteenth Century Venetian Art since 1936. The building lent itself particularly well to a faithful and accurate reproduction of the noble dwellings of the city in that era: For this reason it was restored under the auspices of the city of Venice to house furniture, hangings, carpets and works on the city's history in the 1700s. The palace is thus a luxurious and magnificent record of an historical period and of the life that was lived in houses like this by the patrician families.

There are magnificent Flemish arrasses, valuable furniture, inlaid and engraved by famous masters of the age, such as the work of Andrea Bortolon. The hangings and lamps are of the finest quality, and the rich decoration of the ceilings and plasterwork which adorn vaults and doorways are most striking in their effect.

The rooms of the palace are often further adorned by statues and bas-reliefs. There is a valuable and extensive collection of prints from the eighteenth century, and many fine pictures and frescos.

Some of the paintings are of great importance, notably the work by Gian Battista Tiepolo, entitled *Allegories* (this is to be found in the so-called Throne Room), and his *Strength and Wisdom* (in the Tiepolo Room), and also *The Marriage of Ludovico Rezzonico* in the Room of the Nuptial Allegory.

Among the paintings, a note calls attention to the 34 small pictures by Longhi portraying *Venetian Scenes* - these are exquisite compositions, with remarkable narrative freshness. Famous and typical persons of the Venice of those days are portrayed in them, and they thus provide an insight into the society of the epoch. In the Sala del Ridotto, there are delightful works by Guardi. He also painted some of the ceilings. The female artist Rosalba Carriera is also represented by some interesting works.

17. CHURCH OF SAN SEBASTIANO

Built in the 16th century by Scarpagnino, this is one of Venice's most important churches in its richness and in the value of the paintings which are preserved inside. Some of the most important works of Paolo Veronese, who completely frescoed the walls of the interior, are to be found here. The great Venetian master worked here in the middle years of the sixteenth century, and he also designed the altar and the organ. Among the most notable paintings is *St Mark and St Marcilianus led to execution* (one of the artist's great masterpieces) *The Madonna among Saints, Esther led before Ahasuerus, Esther crowned by Ahasuerus*, and *The Triumph of Mordecai*. In the Sacristy, in the

Church of San Rocco and School of San Rocco.

panels of the ceiling and also on the walls, there are works by Palma the Younger, Andrea Vicentino, Titian and Schiavone. The church is decorated with sculptures by Jacopo Sansovino, pupils of his school, and Girolamo Campagna. The great organ, built in the sixteenth century, is a unique and valuable instrument.

18. CHURCH OF SANT'ANGELO RAFFAELE.

First built in the seventh century, this was then rebuilt in the 17th, and restored again in the 18th. The statue of *the Archangel Raphael* standing above the entrance is Lombard work. The interior, in the form of a Greek cross, is unusual, and there are numerous paintings, among the freshest and most pleasing of the works of the 18th century, by one of the Guardi brothers; the subject is the story of *Tobias and the Angel.*

19. CHURCH OF SAN NICOLÒ DEI MENDICOLI

This is of very ancient origin, dating

perhaps from the seventh century. It was rebuilt in the twelfth century and later transformed. The portico which adorns the facade is from the fifteenth century. The fine Romanesque campanile has graceful trefoil windows in the upper storey.

In the interior much use has been made of discarded material from other buildings, such as the columns which divide the nave. Decoration is provided by paintings of Alvise del Friso, Schiavone and Veronese.

20. CHURCH OF SANTA TERESA

An 18th century building, with paintings from the previous century. It is unusual in being square, and has a coffered ceiling.

21. CHURCH AND SCHOOL OF THE CARMINI (SANTA MARIA DEL CARMELO)

This is an interesting complex from both the architectural and artistic standpoints.

The School is a seventeenth century

building probably designed by Baldassare Longhena. Its fame is linked to the fact that inside it, one of the richest collections of paintings by Tiepolo is to be found. Mention should be made i particular of the *Madonna of the Carmelo*, which gives its name to the building. Among the other artists to be found here are Piazzetta, Padovanino and Balestra.

The Church of Santa Maria del Carmelo has a doorway in the Gothic style, while the remainder of the facade dates from the Renaissance. The interior, divided into three naves by fourteenth century columns and capitals, retains its Gothic form, especially in the architecture of the central nave and the apse.

The decoration is very rich. The central nave has a cycle of paintings of the 17th century: the subject is *Figures and Episodes of the Carmelite Order*. The elaborate screens of gilded wood set between the arches are also of great interest.

Among other works, we may mention the *Adoration of the Shepherds and Saints* painted by Cima da Conegliano in 1509 (2nd altar of the right nave). Along the same nave, after the fourth altar, is an expressive bas-relief representing the *Deposition*, painted by Francesco di Giorgio in the 15th century: The two stalls for cantors on either side of the Presbytery are fine pieces of work, as is the whole wooden choir, adorned with statues of saints. Works of sculpture and painting beautify the apse.

In the left hand nave, at the second altar, there is a fine painting by Lorenzo Lotto, dating from the first years of the 16th century, and featuring *St Nicholas and other saints*, among whom is *St George, killing his dragon*. The charming cloister adjacent to the Church is also worth a visit.

22. CHURCH OF SAN PANTALON

The seventeenth century building designed by Francesco Comino took the place of an earlier, thirteenth century one. The interior has a ceiling painted by G.Antonio Fumiani, with a fresco showing *The Glory of St Pantaleone*. On each side of the single nave there are three chapels, communicating with each other. They are rich in pictorial decoration, which is the work of Fumiani, Veronese, Palma the Younger and Vivarini - the latter represented by a *Coronation of the Blessed Virgin*.

23. CHURCH OF SAN ROCCO AND SCHOOL OF SAN ROCCO

The twin facades of these two buildings look out on to Campo San Rocco, and form a fine architectural complex with scenographical overtones.

CHURCH OF SAN ROCCO

The Church, rebuilt in the 18th century over a previous building in the Renaissance style, has a facade divided into two sections, broken up by Corinthian columns and deep niches with statues. The tympanied doorway is particularly fine, as is the bronze relief in the lunette (a copy of the original by Marchiori). The interior, with a single nave and a dome above the Presbytery, has works by Fumiani, Sebastinao Ricci, Solimena and above all Tintoretto. One of the major works by the latter is the cycle of the *Stories of St Roche*, among which perhaps the most beautiful is *St Roche healing the plague victims*.

GREAT SCHOOL OF SAN ROCCO

This is one of the most interesting of Venice's major architectural complexes. The facade of the building is in two sections, given grace and movement by columns with Corinthian capitals and large two-lancet windows. Built in the fifteenth century for the Confraternity of St Roche (San Rocco), with work by artists including Bartolomeo Bon, Sante Lombardo and Scarpagnino, it is the school which most preserves the cycle of pictures in its interior, the origins of which are in the work of the great master Tintoretto.

Above: *Church of Santa Maria dei Frari.* **Below:** *The Assumption by Titian. Among the many masterpieces collected here, this great canvas by Titian, placed behind the high altar, occupies a position of special importance.*

The painter produced several of his masterpieces here, all characterised by deep expressive qualities. An important role is played by the mobile quality of the figures and scenes, and by the use of colour. The creative intensity which always typified the work of Tintoretto is particularly noticeable in this collection of paintings, which has even caused the School of San Rocco to be compared with the Sistine Chapel. The themes handled by the artist are those of the *Old and New Testaments* and are presented in about sixty paintings, both large and small.

The New Testament scenes include: *The Crucifixion* one of the most dramatic and intense representations of the scene, thanks to the crowded

canvas, the various perspective planes used for the composition, the strong use of shadow, and the explosions of light which make the representation especially vivid. *Jesus before Pilate, the Last Supper, the Prayer in the Garden, the Resurrection, the Baptism, the Nativity, the Temptation of Christ, the Pool of Siloam, the Ascension, the Raising of Lazarus and the Miracle of the Loaves and Fishes*, are the other titles to be seen. The Old Testament scenes depicted are:

Moses causing the water to gush forth; Adam and Eve; God appearing to Moses; Crossing of the Red Sea; Jonah emerging from the belly of the whale; Miracle of the Bronze Serpent; Vision of the Prophet Ezekiel; Jacob's Ladder; The Sacrifice of Isaac; the Fall of the Manna; Elijah supported by the angel; Elijah distributing bread to the people; the Passover of the Jews. We should also mention a Self-portrait of 1573, and paintings of *St Mary Magdalene and St Mary of Egypt*.

In addition, the Scuola di San Rocco has paintings by Titian (*The Annunciation*), by G.B.Tiepolo (*Abraham among the Angels*) and Zanchi (*the Plague of 1630*).

24. CHURCH OF SANTA MARIA DEI FRARI

This was built at the beginning of the fourteenth century, to replace an earlier building which had been assigned to the Franciscan Friars. The building is in brick, with a facade divided into three parts by tall pilasters. In the lower section there is a single elegant doorway, adorned with statues. The campanile, with its trefoil windows in the topmost section, is particularly fine.

The interior is on a grand scale, and there is a solemn severity in the great columns supporting high arches. It has three naves and seven chapels along the end wall of the Presbytery. Along the lateral naves there is a further series of altars.

CENTRAL NAVE:
- *Monument to Titian* (c19th work by the Zandomenghi brothers);
- On the third altar is the statue of *St Jerome* by Alessandro Vittoria;

- *St Catherine* painted by Palma the Younger.

RIGHT WING OF THE TRANSEPT:
- *Monument to Jacopo Marcello* by Pietro Lombardo;
- *Monument of the Blessed Peacemaker*, possibly carved by Nanni di Bartolo; a fine work with rich bas-relief carving;
- *Monument to Benedetto Pesaro*, a Renaissance period work by Lorenzo Bregno and Baccio da Montelupo;
- *Monument to Paolo Savelli*;

SACRISTY:
This is designed in the form of a small church. It was built in the fifteenth century. There are many valuable artworks, including:
- A *Tabernacle of the Relics*, a fine marble and bronze work of the 15th century;

the high altar:
- *Madonna enthroned, with the Child and Saints*, by G.Bellini; one of his finest works.

APSE AND CHAPELS:
- Chapel of St Bernard: it contains a painting by Bartolomeo Vivarini, portraying *The Madonna and Child with Saints*.
- Chapel of the Sacrament: *Tombs of Duccio degli Alberti and Trevisan*, both in the Gothic style.
- Chapel of the Florentines: here the statue of John the Baptist by Donatello is to be found, a wooden carving of great expressive quality. The figure of the Baptist seems to be so cadaverous in body and face that it takes on an intensely agonised and highly dramatic air.
- Presbytery Chapel. Several masterpieces are kept here:
- *The Assumption* by Titian, a great painting in which the movement of the figures is blended and amalgamated by warm and suffusing employment of colour.
- *Monument to Doge Foscari*, work of the Bregno family;
- *Monument to Doge Niccolò Tron*, by Antonio Rizzo in the second half of the fifteenth century; one of the most attractive and harmonious works of the Renaissance.

- Chapel of St Francis: paintings by Palma the Younger, Andrea Vicentino and Bernadino Licinio;
- Trevisan Chapel: this contains fourteenth century wooden statuary, and the *Trevisan Monument* probably by Lorenzo Bregno.
- Chapel of the Milanesi: a fine painting by Alvise Vivarini, depicting *St Ambrose amid angels and saints.*
- Corner Chapel: the chapel dates from the first years of the 15th century; it contains the *Monumnet to Federico Corner*, in the elegant style of the Renaissance.
On the altar is Bartolomeo's painting of *St Mark enthroned bewteen Angels and Saints*
LEFT HAND NAVE:
- Emiliani Chapel: the altar has a marble reredos, decorated with niches and statues.
- *The Madonna di Ca' Pesaro:* another masterpiece by Titian.
- *The Monument of Doge Giovanni Pesaro:* a mausoleum with polychrome marbles and enormous statues. It was carved by Baldassare Longhena.
- *The Monument to Antonio Canova:* designed by the artist himself. It takes the form of a pyramid placed above a staircase: from a rectangular opening the figures of *The Arts*, *St Mark and Genius* enter to pay homage to the artist.
There are other highly prestigious works in this church also: various funeral monuments were built by artists such as Tullio Lombardo, Antonio Rizzo, Bregno and Longhena.

25. CHURCH AND SCHOOL OF SAN GIOVANNI EVANGELISTA

The Church is of fourteenth century origin, but the transformations made in the seventeenth century have profoundly changed its appearance. Inside there are works by Domenico Tintoretto (a *Crucifixion*) Marieschi (*The Last Supper* and *The Exaltation of the Cross*) and Pietro Liberi (*St John the Evangelist*).
The School began life as the home of the Confraternity of the Flagellants of St John, and it is one of the oldest in the city.
The little "campo" (courtyard) of the School is characterised by a marble decoration by Pietro Lombardo; the facade is fifteenth century and is in the Gothic style.
Inside, we find ourselves in spacious Renaissance surroundings: on the ground floor marble objects from the mediaeval period are collected and displayed.
A harmonious staircase designed by the architect Coducci (1498: he was also the designer of the doorway on to the Campiello di San Giovanni) leads to the upper floor, which was transformed in the eighteenth century by Giorgio Massari. There are paintings by Domenico Tiepolo, Sante Parenda, Longhi, Vicentino and Balestra. The altar is by Massari and the statue of St John by Morlaiter.
In the Oratory of Santa Croce, a church decorated with works by Bellini, Carpaccio and others, the "fragment of the Holy Cross" is preserved in a rich golden reliquary. In the Sala dei Convocati are works by Palma the Younger and Guarana.

26. CHURCH OF SAN NICOLÒ DA TOLENTINO

Built by Vincenzo Scamozzi in the 17th century, this church has a fine pronaos by Andrea Tirali, backing on to the still uncompleted facade. The interior has a single nave and a Latin Cross plan. In the midst of florid decorations by 17th and 18th century artists, works by Palma the Younger (a *Madonna and Child with Saints,* and a *Saint Cecilia*) Padovanino (*Episodes in the life of Saint Nicholas*); Bernardo Strozzi (*St Anthony of Padua and St Lorenzo giving gold to the poor*) can be found, together with others by Sante and Luca Giordano, who painted the *Annunciation* situated on the right wall of the Presbytery.

27. SAN SIMEONE PICCOLO

An eighteenth century building, with a typical copper-coloured dome. It has a circular plan; the architect was Scalfarotto, who remodelled it in imitation of the Pantheon.

28. SAN SIMEONE GRANDE

A church of ancient origins completely transformed in the nineteenth century. It has works by Tintoretto and Palma the Younger.

29. CHURCH OF SAN GIACOMO DELL'ORIO

Founded in the ninth century, but rebuilt in both the 13th and 16th, it has a magnificent interior where remains of the ancient basilica can still be seen. The columns that divide the church into naves have different styles and dimensions, and are surmounted by mediaeval capitals. There is a very fine fourteenth century ceiling, which takes the form of the keel of a ship.

There are many artworks: we can find ancient relics, such as the column in the right transept and the capital in the left transept. The paintings by Veronese stand out (some of them decorating the New Sacristy), as do those of Lorenzo Lotto, here represented by a fine *Madonna and Child with Saints*, Palma the Younger, Schiavone, and the Bassanos. Various sculptures and tombs were carved by members of the Lombardo family. The *Crucifix* on board, which hangs at the centre of the Presbytery, is the work of Paolo Veneziano.

30 FONDACO DEI TURCHI AND THE CITY MUSEUM OF NATURAL HISTORY

A fine palazzo in the Venetian-Byzantine style, rebuilt in the 19th century. It is characterised by a series of loggias, one above the other.
It houses the City Museum of Natural History, with collections of great scientific interest, ranging from the entomological section (a very extensive insect collections to that of minerals and fossils. The sectors of marine fauna and ehtnography are particularly well developed. A library dedicated to scientific publications is annexed to the Museum.

31. CHURCH OF SAN STAE

An extremely beautiful baroque construction, built in the first years of the eighteenth century by the architect Domenico Rossi. The facade has tall columns with Corinthian capitals, a grand entrance, a large tympanum and a group of sculptures. The interior tends to the classical and the decoration is mainly eighteenth century. There are many artworks worth seeing, including the *Martyrdom of St Bartholòomew* (a youthful work by Tiepolo) and the *Martyrdom of St James* by Piazzetta.

32. CA' PESARO AND THE GALLERY OF MODERN ART

The Gallery stands on the right bank of the Grand Canal. It was built by Longhena in the 17th century (see section on the Grand Canal). It houses the Gallery of Modern Art and the Oriental Museum.
The Gallery of Modern Art is a very valuable historical collection of the art of the 19th and 20th centuries, with particular attention to trends associated with Venice. At the moment, thanks to its close link with the Biennale it has been broadened to cover the international field.
The artists displayed are among the most prestigious in the world; the most famous work (which was also the Gallery's first acquisition), is Gustav Klint's *Judith* also known as *Salome*.

THE ORIENTAL MUSEUM

Housed on the upper floor of the Ca'Pesaro, it is considered to be one of the largest and most important collections of oriental art in Europe. Begun with materials put together during voyages to the Far East by Henri de Bourbon at the end of the 19th century, the collection has since been augmented by donations from private individuals and corporate bodies.

The Museum has a rich display of armour and weapons, flags and standards, ivories, costumes, sculptures, musical instruments, cloths, ceramics, stones, and figures from the shadow theatre. The collection of screens is exceptional. The countries represented are China, Japan, Indo-China, the Islands of East India, and India itself.

33. THE CHURCH OF SANTA MARIA MATER DOMINI

Built in the sixteenth century, it has a typically well-balanced and harmonious Renaissance appearance. The interior dates from the same period and contains a number of artworks including:
- statues of St Peter and St Paul and of St Mark and St John, by Bregno;
- St Christina amid the Angels a masterpiece by Vincenzo Catena.
- The Discovery of the Holy Cross by Jacopo Tintoretto.

34. THE CHURCH OF SAN CASSIANO

The 17th century building shows some traces of a much older building dating from the tenth century. In the interior, given a particular solemnity by the three naves, all of the same height, there is a splendid Crucifixion by Tintoretto, the effect of which is one of dramatic suffering. There are also a number of paintings by Palma the Younger, Lo Schiavone and GianDomenico Tiepolo.

35. SAN GIOVANNI ELEMOSINARIO

Originating in the 13th century but rebuilt and reordered in later epochs. it has a splendidly elegant interior. Among the artworks there are: St John the Almsgiver by Titian, and St Catherine, St.Sebastian and St Roche by Pordenone (1535).

36. CHURCH OF SAN GIACOMO DI RIALTO

It seems that the origins of this small church date back to the fifth century AD; it was rebuilt in the 16th century, however, by Scarpagnino, after the fire which destroyed it almost completely.

The elegant facade has a characteristic 15th century doorway. The interior, in the form of a Greek cross, has fine columns and capitals which all come from a more ancient building.

37. SAN SILVESTRO

Ancient in origin but entirely rebuilt in the last century. There are many paintings including a very beautiful Baptism of Jesus by Tintoretto.

38. CHURCH OF SANT'APONAL

Built in the fifteenth century in late Gothic style, on the site of an even older church. It is flanked by a bell-tower with trefoil windows in the upper section, and a corona in the Venetian-Byzantine style.

39. PALAZZO ALBRIZZI

A very fine 17th century building, the interior of which is decorated with magnificent stuccos and works by Longhi, Canova Zanchi and Liberi.

40. CHURCH OF SAN POLO

This stands on the wide Campo San Polo, where there are a number of noble houses of the fourteenth and fifteenth centuries. The origins of the Church are ancient, but it was rebuilt in the Gothic style in the 15th century, and subsequently transformed further. The campanile in brick, adorned with marble lions at the base, is, however, original.

In the interior, extensively restored in the 18th century, there are works by Tintoretto (The Last Supper & The Assumption of thge Virgin), G.B.Tiepolo (The Madonna appearing to St John), Paolo Veronese (The Marriage of the Virgin Mary), and Palma the Younger (Conversion of St Paul).

BRIDGE OF SIGHS

(see Itinerary No.1)

1. RIVA DEGLI SCHIAVONI

This is the waterside street that winds along the Basin of San Marco. It gets its nickname from the merchant seamen of Slavonia (this was the name of a region of Dalmatia), who had their trading depot here. The walk offers panoramic views over the Basin of San Marco and leads to the great Arsenal of the City and to the Pavilions of the Biennale. The Riva dei Schiavoni cuts its way through the animated life of the city, amid the crowded cafés which look out over the water, where the gondolas wait, their unmistakable outlines ranked in orderly rows.

2.PALAZZO DANDOLO

Fine building of the fifteenth century decorated with a series of loggias with traceried arches. It is occupied by a hotel where in the past musicians, writers and princes have stayed.

3. PALAZZO TREVISAN

The Renaissance building has a facade with graceful windows and polychrome medallion decoration.

4. CHURCH OF SAN GIULIANO

Probably originating in the 9th century, it was rebuilt in the sixteenth by Jacopo Sansovino and Vittoria. On the facade, divided up by columns and embellished by statues, the most notable feature is a

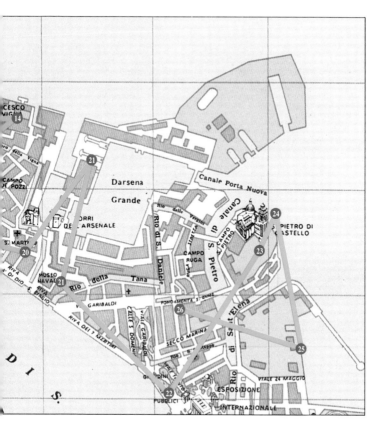

bronze of *Tommaso Rangone*.. The interior is rich in paintings and sculptures; one of the most outstanding works being the *Pietà* by Girolamo Campagna.

5. PALAZZO QUERINI-STAMPALIA AND QUERINI-STAMPALIA LIBRARY AND ART GALLERY

Both the Library and the Art Gallery were private property until the nineteenth century. Subsequently, with the creation of the Querini-Stampalia Foundation they were given to the City.

The Library is rich in incunabula and manuscripts of great value.

The Art Gallery is dispersed among twenty or so rooms of the palazzo. Some of the finest masterpieces of Venetian art are preserved there, beginning with the fourteenth century and running to the end of the eighteenth. The painting of Longhi is particularly well represented. Among the most important artists are Lorenzo di Credi (*Madonna*), Giovanni Bellini (*Presentation in the Temple*), Palma the Elder (*Sacred Conversation*),Palma the Younger (to whom a whole room is dedicated), G.B.Tiepolo (*a portrait*), Schiavone and Vincenzo Catena.

6. CHURCH OF SANTA MARIA FORMOSA

It has a seventeenth century facade and a harmonious interior from the fifteenth century, built by Coducci. It contains works by Bartolomeo Vivarini, Leandro Bassano and a fine painting by Palma the Younger, portraying St *Barbara*, to whom the Church was formerly dedicated.

7. MONUMENT TO COLLEONI

The equestrian group is to be found at the centre of the Campo di San Giovanni e Paolo. It is one of the greatest of all masterpieces of Renaissance art. It was carved by Verrocchio towards the end of the fifteenth century. The composition is highly expressive in its moral energy which derives from the frowning expression and fierce pride to be found in the great condottiere's features.

8. CHURCH OF SAN GIOVANNI E PAOLO, KNOWN AS ZANIPOLO.

Together with the Basilica of San Marco and the Frari, this is one of the most significant artistic centres in Venice. The Church was built in the 13th century for the Dominican Order, and was only completed in the mid-fifteenth century.

Exterior

Its typical features are the use of brick and the elegant simplicity of the Gothic facade. The lower part of this facade is broken up by blind arches in which funeral monuments have been inserted. At the centre is the great doorway, outlined by marble columns, the work of Bartolomeo Bon.

The apsidal section is particularly beautiful; here the play of volumes created by the polygonal design is aided by magnificent double-lancet windows.

Interior

This is divided into three naves, by tall columns surmounted by pointed arches. It is particularly rich in art works:

At the rear of the facade:

- *Monument of the Doge Alvise Mocenigo*;
- *Monument of the Doge Pietro Mocenigo*, an exceptional work by Pietro Lombardo (15th century);

Right-hand nave:

- On the 1st Altar is the *Madonna and Child and Saints* by Francesco Bissolo, set in a carved frame of bas-reliefs.

- *Monument to Antonio Bragadin* carved by Scamozzi and dedicated to one of the heroes of Venice.

- 2nd Altar: a fine polyptich, portraying St Vincent Ferreri, one of the earliest works of Giovanni Bellini;

Church of San Giovanni e Paolo. The Church is also known as San Zanipolo.

- Chapel of the Addolorata: this is in the Gothic style and was decorated with stuccos in the 17th century;
- Chapel of the Madonna della Pace, so-called from the Byzantine image of Our Lady on the Altar;
- Chapel of San Domenico; the roof of this chapel is dominated by the large painting of the *Glories of* St.Do-

minic, one of the best works by Piazzetta (1727).
- *Christ* by Alvise Vivarini;
- *The Almsgiving of St Anthony*, by Lorenzo Lotto (16th century);
- Chapel of the Crucifix: there are funerary monuments and statues in bronze by Vittoria;
- Chapel of the Maddalena, in the Renaissance style.

Presbytery:
- The High Altar is a masterpiece by Longhena;
- Funerary Monuments of Venetian Doges, among them that to Andrea Vendramin, the work of Pietro and Antonio Lombardo.
- Chapel of the Trinity: here there are a number of tombs, some of them pensile in design.
- Cavalli Chapel.
Left Transept:
Here there are Funerary Monuments: that of Doge Antonio Venier has carvings by Pierpaolo Dalle Masegne.
- Chapel of the Rosary: this is a treasurehouse of works of art. There are paintings by Veronese, depicting The Annunciation, the Adoration and the Assumption, and others by Bonifacio de'Pitati. In addition the Chapel contains sculptures by Alessandro Vittoria and Girolamo Campagna.
Left-hand nave:
- Sacresty: works by Bassano and Vicentino;
- Monument of Doge Pasquale Malpiero;
- Monument of Doge Tommaso Mocenigo (the work of Franco Terilli da Feltre);
- Monument to Doge Nicolò Marcello, by Pietro Lombardo,
- Statue by Alessandro Vittoria, portraying St Jerome.

9. CHURCH OF THE MIRACLES

The church is in the Renaissance style, and was built by Pietro Lombardo in the early 16th century. The facade is divided into two sectors by semi-columns interrupted by architraves on the lower level and ending in arches in the upper part. The interior has a single nave, with rich marble decoration. The coffered ceiling, and in particular the marble bas-reliefs and the traceried screens which are to be found in the presbytery are worthy of special note. The Lombardos, Alessandro Vittoria and Girolamo Campagna all contributed to the sculptures.

10. CHURCH OF SAN CANCIANO

The Church owes its present appearance to the eighteenth century. Inside there are paintings and stucco decorations.

11. GREAT SCHOOL OF SAN MARCO

A Renaissance building designed by Pietro Lombardo, and in the upper part by Mauro Coducci. It has an unusual facade in polychrome marble. The construction is assymmetrical, and has a large decorated doorway and pointed windows with tympana. The front is crowned with a series of arches of varying heights.
In the interior - now used as the City Hospital - some of the rooms have fine wooden ceilings, formerly with paintings by Bellini and Carpaccio (these works have been transferred to the Gallery of the Accademia).

12. CHURCH OF SAN LAZZARO DEI MENDICANTI

Designed by Scamozzi in the first years of the 17th century, it has several works by Tintoretto (the painting on the first altar on the left, depicting the Stories of St Ursula is especially fine) and by Veronese.

13. CHURCH OF THE OSPEDALETTO

Designed by Longhena in the second half of the 17th century, it has a superabundance of marble decoration. The interior has a rich variety of paintings from the 17th century.

14. CHURCH OF SAN FRANCESCO DELLA VIGNA

Legend has it that St Mark himself landed at the place where the church stands. It has a facade in the Palladian style, dating from the mid 16th century.
The interior has to a great extent

School of San Marco. The church stands on the small Campo di San Marco, in one of the most evocative corners of Venice.

preserved the appearance given to it by the original design of Jacopo Sansovino. There are a number of important artworks, including:
- The Giustiniani Chapel, where the sculptures are by Pietro Lombardo;
- a *Madonna and Child* by Giovanni Bellini (1507);
- a *Madonna and Child with Saints*, a very fine painting by Antonio da Negroponte; as well as these, sculptures by Longhena and Vittoria, and paintings by Vivarini, Veronese and Tiepolo are also to be found.

15. CHURCH OF SAN GIORGIO DEI GRECI

Built in the sixteenth century, this Church is in Renaissance style and was designed by Sante Lombardo. The interior has Byzantine paintings and a wooden Choir.

16. SCHOOL OF SAN GIORGIO DEI SCHIAVONI

Built in the 16th century, it has a facade after the manner of Sansovino, but designed in fact by Giovanni De Zan for the Dalmatian community. It is of primary importance because of the very beautiful cycle painted by Vittore Carpaccio (first years of the 16th century).
These works, which have a remarkable narrative freshness and a scrupulous attention to detail, were painted with exceptional creativity.
They depict *Stories of St George and St Jerome*. Among these, the most outstanding are *St George and the Dragon* and *St Augustine in his study*. There are also *Episodes from the life of St Tryphon*, and subjects from the Gospels.

17. CHURCH OF SAN ZACCARIA

This is one of Venice's most interesting churches. The story of its construction is somewhat complex; built in the ninth century, it was reconstructed in the thirteenth, and then transformed again in the fourteenth and fifteenth centuries. The splendid facade is divided into sections marked out by loggias set one above the other, with pointed arches and niches.

The interior is divided into three naves: its elegant, perfectly balanced architecture creates an immediate effect, as do the complex structural relations and the mixture of styles.

There are many masterpieces among the works preserved here:
- *two holy water stoups*, decorated with statues of St *John and St Zachariah* by Alessandro Vittoria;
- *The Glory of St Zachariah* by Palma the Younger (the artist has used a series of small paintings for this theme);
- *The Adoration of the Shepherds* one of the finest works by Antonio Balestra;
- *The Birth of St John Baptist* by Tintoretto;
- *Tobias healing his father* by Bernardo Strozzi;
- *Madonna enthroned, with the Child*, by Giovanni Bellini;
- Chapel of San Tarasio: splendid triptychs and a painting depicting *The Birth of St John Baptist*, by Andrea del Castagno;
- fragments of a mosaic pavement from the former building.

18. CHURCH OF THE PIETÀ

This church was built in the eighteenth century. The interior, with its oval plan, is one of the most important examples of the architecture of this century. A row of marble semicolumns with Corinthian capitals follows the internal perimeter of the Church, which is given additional movement by eight lateral chapels. The decorations and paintings by Tiepolo are also noteworthy, especially the *Coronation of Mary*, which occupies the ceiling of the nave, and dates from the mid 1700s. There are also paintings by Piazzetta and statues by Morlaiter and Marchiori.

19. CHURCH OF SAN GIOVANNI IN BRAGORA

This has a late Gothic facade, built in the second half of the fifteenth century.

The interior, divided into three naves, has preserved the Venetian Gothic style almost intact, even though the building underwent restoration in the 18th century.

There are many interesting works of art, including:
- *The Baptism of Christ* by Cima da Conegliano (late 15th century);
- A triptych depicting the *Madonna and Child* by Bartolomeo Vivarini (left hand nave);
- Small paintings on wood by Jacobelle da Fiore;
- *Christ rising from the dead*, by Alvise Vivarini, the nephew of Bartolomeo;
- *Tha Last Supper* by Paris Bordone;
- The *Baptismal Font*, hollowed out of a Gothic capital;
- *Madonna and Child*, a bas-relief of Venetian Byzantine workmanship.

20. CHURCH OF SAN MARTINO

It was designed by Sansovino and built in the last years of the 16th century, but subsequently transformed. The fine doorway is all that remains of the elegant architecture of the Renaissance church.

The interior, which has a Greek cross plan with chapels added, houses a number of paintings by Zanchi. The unusual baptismal font is a work of the Lombard period.

21. THE ARSENAL - MUSEUM OF NAVAL HISTORY

The Arsenal was built in the first

years of the eleventh century, and consists of a large group of buildings and dockyards which have played a major part over the centuries in the history and fortunes of the Venetian Republic.

The first building was erected in 1104 on the orders of Doge Ordelaffo Valier. It was then enlarged in the 14th century, and again in the 15th and 16th, in order to respond to the growing needs of the city which, as Queen of the Seas, sent its ships to every part of the world, and especially to the Far East. In 1579 the so-called *Tana* was built, i.e. the three-nave building where all types of ropework for boats and ships waas produced.

The entry to the Arsenal from the landward side, in the form of a triumphal arch, should be noted. This is a work of the Renaissance architect Antonio Gambello.

In what was once the ancient granary, the **Museum of Naval History** is now housed; it is one of the largest of its kind. It contains 25,000 items, providing full information on all types of ship, on arms, anchors and naval equipment. There is an exceptional exhibit of model ships, the most interesting of all being the *Bucintoro*.

22. PUBLIC GARDENS INTERNATIONAL EXHIBITION OF MODERN ART

For many years now, these pavilions have housed the Biennale, the two yearly exhibition of contemporary art. Every nation has its own building where it puts on display the works of its major artists, and the most significant stylistic developments.

23. THE ISLAND OF SAN PIETRO

Separated from the other islands by the Canale San Pietro and the Canale Sant'Elena, it was one of the first settlements in the lagoon. It is a secluded, silent and tranquil corner of the city, inhabited mainly by fishermen.

24. CHURCH OF SAN PIETRO DI CASTELLO

The ancient cathedral of the city, which originated in the 8th century, but was constantly renovated and transformed. The interior haas been redesigned according to the Palladian style.

There are numerous artworks, including some which belong to the original building. Pictorial decoration, however, is mostly from the baroque period.

Worth a mention is the *Throne of St Peter*, a thirteenth century work which used material of Arabic origins, as can be seen from the inscriptions which are in fact quotations from the Koran.

The high altar designed by Longhena is particularly fine, as is the Vedramin Chapel in the left wing of the transept.

25. ISLAND OF SANT'ELENA

Linked by a bridge to the other islands, it is dominated by the church of the same name, of thirteenth century origins but completely renovated in subsequent centuries.

The facade has a fine main doorway and a marble group by Antonio Rizzo, dating from the late fifteenth century.

The general lines of the interior still keep their Gothic form.

26. CHURCH OF SAN FRANCESCO DI PAOLA

This still keeps its simple fifteenth century facade, while the interior was remodelled in the 18th century.

The decorations are from that period (by G.B.Tiepolo, Contarini, and Marieschi).

1. CHURCH OF SAN MOISÈ

The Church dedicated to Moses has a sumptuous facade in the baroque style by Alessandro Tremignon, built for Moisè Venier. The campanile still retains its fourteenth century features. The interior is also baroque in arrangement and decoration. The paintings date mostly from the seventeenth and eighteenth centuries, though a few works are by Tintoretto and Palma the Younger.

2. CHURCH OF SANTA MARIA ZOBENIGO

The church traces its origins back to the ninth century, but was rebuilt in the seventeenth, as witness the facade with its abundant statuary. Inside, there are paintings by Domenico Tintoretto, Rubens (attributed - *The Holy Family*),Palma the Younger, Zanchi and Jacopo Tintoretto. (*The Evangelists*).

80

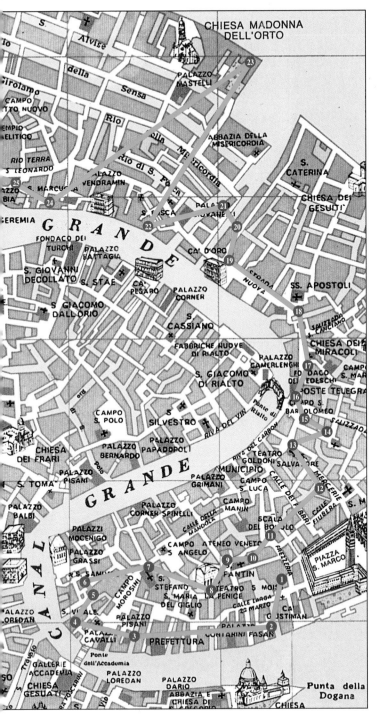

3. PALAZZO PISANI

An eighteenth century building with typical rustication and large arched windows of the Serlian type. The interior, with its sumptuous stucco decoration, is of great elegance.

4. CHURCH OF SAN VITALE

The seventeenth century building took the place of an earlier 12th century one. It was designed by Tirali, and the facade has echoes of the Palladian style.

5. PALAZZO LOREDAN

This was designed by Scarpagnino, in a harmonious Renaissance style.

6. CHURCH OF SAN SAMUELE

Originally founded in the ninth century - and the fine portico from that period still survives - the church was rebuilt in the seventeenth. The small twelfth century campanile in the Romanesque style is original, however.
The interior has a Gothic apse and the Byzantine icon of the *Madonna* which is considered to be miraculous.

7. CHURCH OF SANTO STEFANO

This is one of the best examples of Gothic architecture in the city. The brick facade has a fifteenth centu-

---

Church of San Moisè.

La Fenice Theatre: *view of the interior, now completely destroyed by fire.*

ry doorway by Bartolomeo Bon. The traceried windows are very delicate.

The interior has three naves and a pitched roof. A row of columns with painted capitals upholds high-pitched arches. On the floor can be seen the tombstone of Doge Francesco Morosini. Among the numerous artworks, we should mention paintings by Jacopo Tintoretto, Paris Bordone, Piazzetta and Vivarini. There is a fine apse where the large High Altar has statues by Campagna. It is especially worth while to visit the attractive Cloister, probably designed by Scarpagnino.

8. LA FENICE THEATRE

One of the most prestigious theatres in Italy. It was built at the end of the eighteenth century in the neo-classical style. In 1995 it was tragically destroyed by a fire, and is now in process of reconstruction.

9. SCHOOL OF SAN GIROLAMO AND SAN FANTIN

Here the Venetian Athenaeum has its headquarters. In the building there are paintings by Antonio Zanchi (17th century).

10. CHURCH OF SAN FANTIN

A harmonious building in the Renaissance style, built initially by Scarpagnino and added to by Sansovino. The interior, notable for its elegant architecture and its very well-balanced structural design, has a nave with slender pilasters flanked by semicolumns supporting arches and a cross vaulted ceiling.

11. SCALA A BOVOLO - PALAZZO CONTARINI DEL BOVOLO

This is an unusual staircase attached to the Palazzo Contarini-Bovolo, built in the fifteenth century by Giovanni Candi. The architetcural structure is based on a cylindrical construction open on the outside, and an arcade which rises in spiral form; inside there is a spiral staircase. The elegant marble dressing of the arches stands out against the brick frontage of the building.

12. THE MERCERIE

This is the busy centre of the city. It links Piazza San Marco to the Grand Canal, cutting directly across the built-up area.

The name derives from the numerous small shops which are to be found on both sides of the street.

13. CHURCH OF SAN SALVATORE

Ancient in foundation, the church has been transformed numerous times; its present aspect is due to the work of Tullio Lombardo initially, later modified by Scamozzi (16th century). In the 17th century the baroque facade was added.

The interior is interesting both for its graceful Renaissance architecture and for a number of important paintings:

- *The Annunciation*, a splendid work by Titian, and one of his last;
- *The Supper at Emmaus*: a masterpiece by Giovanni Bellini, which makes a great impact by means of colour and light;
- *Hope* by Sansovino;
- *The Transfiguration*, painted by Titian in 1560
- the splendid altarpiece in silver and gold, carved in the fourteenth century (High Altar);
- sculptural groups by Girolamo Campagna decorate the *funerary monument* near the first altar on the right.

14. CHURCH OF SAN LIO

The church was originally dedicated to St Catherine. Its present aspect derives from the reconstruction of the eighteenth century. The interior has a fine roof, with frescoes by Domenico Tiepolo. The Gussoni Chapel is a Renaissance period work by Pietro Lombardo.

15. CAMPO SAN BARTOLOMEO AND CHURCH OF SAN BARTOLOMEO

The 18th century restoration has completely transformed the original twelfth century structure.

The interior is divided into three naves separated by columns. Among the artworks are those of Sebastiano del Piombo (*St Sebast-*

ian and St Bartholemew, dating from the 16th century), Palma the Younger, Sante Perenda and Tintoretto.

16. FONDACO DEI TEDESCHI

A building in the Renaissance style, designed by Scarpagnino. The front looks out over the Grand Canal; in the lower section it has a portico, while on the upper floor there are two loggias. At one time it was decorated with paintings by Tintoretto and Giorgione, but these have been lost.

17. CHURCH OF SAN GIOVANNI CRISOSTOMO

Originating in the 9th century, this was completely rebuilt in the 15th and 16th centuries. The facade shows the simple and harmonic lines of the Renaissance style.

The interior is of the same style and period, notable for its well-balanced structure and for the magnificent cycle of paintings:

1st Altar: *St Christopher, St Jerome and St Augustine*: this is one of the most important works by Giovanni Bellini;

2nd Altar: *Passage of St Joseph*, by Carlo Loth (17th century);

Apse: High Altar: *St John Chrysostom and other saints*, a masterpiece by Sebastiano del Piombo.

18. CHURCH OF SS APOSTOLI

The church has undergone several major restorations, the most important of which were in the sixteenth and eighteenth centuries.

The interior dates from the sixteenth century. It has a single nave with altars along the walls. Among the works to be found here are *The Communion of Saint Lucia*. by G.B.Tiepolo, and a Byzantine fresco in the right hand chapel of the Presbytery. The Corner Chapel where the *Tomb of Marco Corner*, probably by Tullio Lombardo, is to be found, is of great beauty.

Campo San Bartolomeo.

19. THE CA' D'ORO - GALLERIA FRANCHETTI

The building owes its splendour to the wonderful blending of architectural and decorative elements, the chromatic beauty of its surfaces and the very delicate filigree work which accompanies the structural elements. Referred to as the "Golden House" because of the gilding which once covered its surfaces, the Palazzo is one of the finest examples of Venetian Gothic architecture of the fifteenth century. The entry courtyard and a second courtyard beyond it are in the same elegant style as the exterior. In the centre of the main courtyard is a magnificent wellhead by Bartolomeo Bon.

The Galleria Franchetti in the Ca' d'Oro.

This rich and extremely important collection of paintings includes a section with medals, seals, tapestries, ceramics and period furniture.The Gallery is housed in rooms on the first and second floors. Among the most outstanding works we find:

- Saint Sebastian, a masterpiece by Mantegna (1506);
- *Portrait of a Gentleman*, a highly refined and expressive work by van Dyck;
- *Portrait of a Young Girl*, one of Pontormo's most important works with its exceptional rendering of the girl's inner life through her physical features;
- *Venus at the Mirror*, by Titian;
- *St Mark's Square* and *View of the Wharf and the Salute Point*, two of Francesco Guardi's most evocative views of Venice;
- *The Birth of Jesus*, a tender painting by Filippino Lippi;
- Works by Paris Bordone, Cima da Conegliano, Domenico and Jacopo Tintoretto, Domenico Ghirlandaio, Andrea di Bartolo, Giovanni Bellini and , among the sculptors, Jacopo Sansovino, Alessandro Vittoria and Pietro Lombardo.

Works by Pisanello among the remarkable collection of the *Medagliere* must certainly be mentioned.

20. CHURCH OF SAN FELICE

A 16th century church built on severely Renaissance lines. Its attractive interior contains works by Tintoretto and other artists.

21. PALAZZO GIOVANELLI

It has a handsome Gothic facade decorated with filigree windows.

22. CHURCH OF SANTA FOSCA

Dating from very ancient times the church was completely rebuilt in the 17th century. The fine bell-tower decorated with filigree windows in the upper part was built in the 15th century.

Inside we find works painted by Carlo Loth and Domenico Tintoretto.

23. CHURCH OF THE MADONNA DELL'ORTO

This is one of the most interesting churches in Venice. It is named after the statue of the Madonna inside, which is considered to be miraculous: it was found in a field close to the church. The magnificent terra-cotta facade combines features of the Romanesque, Gothic and Renaissance. The remarkable trefoiled loggia motive follows the line of the sloping roof with statues of the Apostles set in the niches. The ornamentation on the great doorway is of exceptional quality.

Inside, the three naves are divided by marble columns supporting terra-cotta arches.

The church contains numerous works of art of great renown. Outstanding is the amazing panel by Cima da Conegliano showing *St John the Baptist among the Saints* (15th century).

We also find one of Tintoretto's absolute masterpieces : *The Presentation of Mary in the Temple* which he painted in 1552. Again by Tintoretto there are his beautiful *Last Judgment* and the *Adoration of the Golden Calf* (presbytery).

Above the altars we find works by Palma the Younger and Giovanni Bellini.

24. CHURCH OF SAN MARCUOLA

This 18th century building designed by Giorgio Massari has an interesting square-plan interior with pairs of side chapels and surfaces articulated with half columns.

Among the works of art we find 17th century paintings by Francesco Migliori, and a beautiful *Last Supper* by Jacopo Tintoretto painted when he was a young man (second half of the 16th century).

25. PALAZZO LABIA

One of the most sumptuous Venetian palaces. It was built in the 18th century by Andrea Cominelli with a magnificent facade, rusticated on the ground floor and decorated with two orders of half columns on the upper storeys.

The palace is famous for a cycle of frescoes with elaborate and highly realistic perspectives painted by G. B. Tiepolo in the second half of the 18th century. The various subjects range from historical episodes such as *Antony and Cleopatra* and allegorical representations of *Time, Beauty* and *Genius*.

26. CHURCH OF SAN GIOBBE

The church was built in Renaissance style in the 15th century above an Oratory where San Bernardino of Siena once lived. It has a richly decorated entrance door.

The single nave interior is embellished with interesting works of art, including Antonio Vivarini's spectacular triptych of the *Annunciation* in the da Mula chapel.

The *Presepe* by Savoldo also deserves attention. This 16th century work stands above the altar in the

Church of the Madonna dell'Orto. The magnificent facade is characterised by a Loggetta in marble decorated with statues.

Gothic Contarini chapel.

The remarkableRenaissance Presbytery is one of the masterpieces of Pietro Lombardo. Also of interest is the Chapel of the Virgin, one of the rare examples of Tuscan art in Venice. Here we find terra-cotta works by Della Robia.

27. CHURCH OF SAN GEREMIA

The original church on this site can be traced back to the 13th century, but it was mostly rebuilt in the 18th century, and the facade in the 19th century. Its 13th century bell-tower is particurlarly beautiful.

The interior follows the Greek cross plan with a central dome and long slender columns.

28. CHURCH OF THE SCALZI

This is the name given to the church of Santa Maria di Nazareth built by Baldassarre Longhena in the 17th century for the Order of Discalced Carmelites. The beautiful Baroque facade is adorned with a series of statues, niches, paired columns and a magnificent entrance.

The sumptuous interior is rich in polychrome marble, statues and busts, with Baroque altars beneath baldachins. Here we find the *Tomb* of Ludovico Manin, last of the Venetian Doges.

The paintings come mostly from the 17th and 18th centuries. There is a very fine fresco of *Santa Teresa* by G. B. Tiepolo.

ENVIRONS OF VENICE THE VENETIAN LAGOON

The Venetian lagoon is composed of a group of islands and places of natural interest which are a great attraction for tourists. It is also exceptionally beautiful. The Lido, and the islands of Burano, Murano and Torcello certainly have great appeal for the visitor as well as winding up his overall knowlege of Venice. Apart from monuments of world renown there are spots where a few moments of peace and quiet can be found, as well as wonderful views and attractive comfortable beaches along the shores of the Adriatic. In the pretty little towns and villages on the islands we can discover traditions that go back thousands of years and reveal the extraordinary skill and creativity of the inhabitants: the art of glass blowing is mainly practiced on Murano and is the most striking example of the work of master-craftsmen who have created an authentic art form over the centuries.

Then there is the lace-work of Burano, patiently and expertly produced by the women of the island: this too has become one of the most valued expressions of artistic craftsmanship. The Lido, the long island which almost completely closes the Venetian lagoon from the sea, is famous for its fashionable beaches, and particularly for its important cultural events.

LIDO

This is the name of the long strip of land separating Venice from the open sea. Two channels divide it from the other land barriers along the shores of the lagoon: the San Nicolò channel and the one at Alberoni. The Lido is in the forefront of tourist attractions because of its splendid and elegantly equipped beach facilities, as well as for the important international cultural events held there. Among these the **International Exhibition of the Art of Cinema,** or the Venice Film Festival, must be mentioned. We also find here the Municipal **Casino.**

The Lido has been inhabited since the Middle Ages.The **Benedictine Monastery of San Nicolò** was founded there in 1044. The small village of the same name has grown up around it. The Lido is in easy reach of the charming village of **Malomocco** huddled around its small central square. It was founded in the 6th century on the opposite shore of the island by Venetians who were fleeing from invasion, and rebuilt a few centuries later on its present site.

In front of the Lido port stands the **Fortress of Sant' Andrea** built in the 16th century by the architect Sanmicheli.

Palazzo of the International Film Festival
Panorama of the Venice Lido

Panoramic view of the Lido of Venice.

MURANO

This is the best known of the islands in the lagoon and its fame comes from the production of exquisite glass-work which has reached an extraordinarily high level of artistry.

The craft of glass blowing has been carried out for centuries and in every period has expressed the consummate skill and creativity of innumerable masters. A Glass **Museum** documents this splendid tradition. A visit to the glass works completes one's knowlege of this ancient art which has been carried out under the most refined methods known to the craft.

The island of Murano is also fascinating for its churches and palaces which reflect the architectural splendour of the ones in Venice.

Particularly handsome are the Gothic **Palazzo da Mula**, the **Palazzo Giustinian** and the Palladian **Palazzo Trevisan**.

A visit should also be made to the Renaissance **Church of San Pietro Martire** where we can admire works by Giovanni Bellini (*Madonna and Child with Saints*) and Paolo Veronese (*St Jerome in the Desert*). There are very fine wooden dossals in the Sacristy.

The **church of Santa Maria e Donato** goes back to very ancient times.

It was founded in the 7th century, but rebuilt in the 12th century. The apse is particularly beautiful with its double order of terra-cotta loggias whose arches are bordered with marble. The bell-tower is 13th century.

The interior of the church has three naves divided by columns with magificent capitals. The 12th century floor is paved with beautiful mosaics. Here we find works of art like the Pala of *San Donato* by Paolo Veneziano.

Like Venice the island of Murano has a Grand Canal of its own, flanked by stately buildings of the finest architecture.

Above: Basilica of Saints Maria and Donato.
Below: One of the glass manufacturies which have made Murano famous throughout the world.

BURANO

Burano is very picturesque with its pretty little painted houses along the small canals that intersect the island. Here we can find unforgettable spots with a charming atmosphere.

Burano has preserved the look of a typical fishing village. Fishing boats make their way along the canals that criss-cross the island and the nets are hung out along the embankments. The island is really four tightly connected islets. It was populated when barbarian invasions drove the Venetians on to the lagoon where they found a place that was naturally sheltered and secure.

The fame of the island of Burano is linked to the production of lace which the women of Burano work with consummate skill. It is a tradition that has passed down through the centuries and finds its expression in products of exquisite beauty and elegance. Begun in the 16th century at the command of the wives of some of the Doges, lace-making has been cultivated with patience and a remakable sense of artistry. The **Lace School** was created to preserve this art.

The 16th century church of **San Martino** well deserves a visit.

In the 17th century **church of Santa Barbara** there is a beautiful painting by Giovan Battista Tiepolo of "The Calvary".

Venetian Lagoon: Burano. The island has preserved a remarkable atmosphere of the past and is also famous for the exquisite lace proudly and skillfully worked by the women of the island.

TORCELLO

A delightful island in the Venetian lagoon, an oasis of peace and stillness.

The **Cathedral of Santa Maria Assunta** dates from the 7th century and was rebuilt a number of times. Its architecture is a typical example of the Ravenna style. The facade is preceded by a narthex. Beside it we find remains of an ancient baptistry with an octagonal plan.

The interior has three naves divided by marble columns supporting magnificent 11th century capitals.

A great mosaic covers the west wall showing the Last Judgment (Byzantine work of the 12th century). The Iconostasis in front of the Presbytery is particularly fine: it contains 13 icons showing the Madonna and 12 Apostles and some sculptures. There is a magnificent mosaic in the vault of the apse showing the Madonna and Child (13th century).

CHURCH OF SANTA FOSCA

Built in the 11th century on an octagonal plan. It is preceded by a portico that occupies 5 sides of the building. The interior architecture is remarkable for its harmonious amalgamation of the Greek cross plan with the articulation of the apses.

ISLAND OF SAN LAZZARO DEGLI ARMENI

On the island visitors can see the rich Library, a printing press, the Art Gallery and Sculpture Museum which also contains memorabilia of Lord Byron who used to stay here.

Torcello: The Last Judgment - a marvellous mosaic which occupies the interior facade of the Church of Santa Maria Assunta.
Following page: Church of Santa Maria Assunta.

INDEX

ENGLISH VERSION BY BRIAN WILLIAMS & ADRIAN COOK
PHOTO: ARCHIVIO PLURIGRAF - CAMERAPHOTO-ARTE - DAL MAGRO - BARONE - ARTE VIDEO